# A VOICE CRYING IN THE WILDERNESS

# A VOICE CRYING IN THE WILDERNESS
## THE LIFE & MINISTRY OF JOHN THE BAPTIST

### KEITH S. HODGES

© 2017 by Keith S. Hodges

All rights reserved. No part of this publication may be reproduced, stored in a retrieval system, or transmitted in any form or by any means without the prior written permission of the author. The only exception is brief quotations in printed reviews.

ISBN-10: 1944704493
ISBN-13: 978-1944704490

Published by Start2Finish Books
Fort Worth, Texas 76244
www.start2finish.org

Printed in the United States of America

Unless otherwise noted, all Scripture quotations are from Revised Standard Version of the Bible, copyright © 1946, 1952, and 1971 National Council of the Churches of Christ in the United States of America. Used by permission. All rights reserved worldwide.

Cover Design: Josh Feit, Evangela.com

I dedicated my first book, *The Simon Peter Principles*, to my wonderful father and mother, Lee and Kay Hodges. Since then they have both departed this life, leaving a wonderful legacy of faith, hard work, happy living, loving family and friends, and helping people.

I am now delighted to dedicate this second book to my loving wife, Francie. She became the "wife of my youth" in 1971, and has been my constant companion, counselor, encourager, and sometimes loving critic. She is also a wonderful mother and grandmother. Her quiet strength and service is appreciated around this country and beyond.

# CONTENTS

*Prologue*   9
*Introduction*   11

1. Front Man — 17
2. Rugged Individualism — 21
3. Background — 25
4. John Is Elijah? — 29
5. Prepare the Way — 33
6. Joy & Gladness — 37
7. Talked About — 41
8. In the Wilderness — 45
9. A Man Sent from God — 49
10. Not the Light Chapter — 53
11. He Came Preaching — 57
12. Repent! — 61
13. A Special Baptism — 65
14. John Bearing Witness — 69
15. Transferring Disciples — 73

| 16. | Continuing for a While | 77 |
| 17. | From a Different Viewpoint | 81 |
| 18. | Evil Outdoing Itself | 85 |
| 19. | Fear That Doesn't Repent | 89 |
| 20. | Why This Question, Now? | 93 |
| 21. | None Greater Than John | 97 |
| 22. | The Opportunity for Evil | 101 |
| 23. | Deep Respect | 105 |
| 24. | The Aftermath of a Great Life | 109 |
| 25. | Similarities to Jesus | 113 |
| 26. | Jesus on John | 117 |
| 27. | Christ Superseding | 121 |
| 28. | Knew Only John's Baptism | 125 |
| | *Epilogue* | 129 |
| | *Acknowledgments* | 135 |

# PROLOGUE

> *"Truly, I say to you, among those born of women there has arisen no one greater than John the Baptist. Yet the one who is least in the kingdom of heaven is greater than he."* (Matt. 11:11)

This statement by Jesus is typical of several ironies we can find regarding one of the Bible's most fascinating characters, John the Baptist. The irony includes the fact that the one making the statement is, without a doubt, the greatest person who ever lived. Then the irony continues in Jesus' statement that whomever would be the least in the kingdom would be greater than John the Baptist. That includes potentially you or me. How can any of us, who hopefully realize our weaknesses and failures, even begin to compare in greatness to this man? In this book we'll explore these and many other intriguing things about a rather mysterious but powerful figure in the story of the gospel.

I am definitely one of those who think John the Baptist is the second greatest person who ever lived. I didn't come to that conclusion easily, especially in light of such Biblical heroes as Abraham, Moses, David, Elijah, Mary, Peter, John, and Paul. I had that conviction before

I started writing this book, and it has only grown and intensified since then.

John the Baptist's greatness is not because of the length of his life and ministry, nor how much of the Bible's text was written by or about him. Neither was this man's greatness just because of the nature and timing of his ministry. Rather it is because of the humility and faithfulness with which he fulfilled the role God had given him.

The amount of information, the specifics regarding John the Baptist, is scant compared to other key biblical figures. If you're like me, you may find yourself saying, "I want to know more!" What might seem like gaps in his story to us arises from having more we'd like to read about him from the Scriptures. Many would love more about how he came to have the faith, courage, and humility we see in him. We're not told how he felt after certain great events in his life. We see him, like so many Bible characters simply acting out of great faith, a faith we trust had been carefully forged over time and diligently maintained.

The best interpretation of John the Baptist's attitude and actions, as well as any speculation we might make will have to be found in biblical passages not directly about him. We'll have to, in effect, color in what we can from the wonderful array of biblical principles and accounts about godliness and service, and how God acts providentially in the lives of His servants.

I invite you to join with me in the consideration of this outstanding biblical character whose light shone briefly but so brightly. His light shines on now and into eternity because of the proficiency with which he fulfilled his vital ministry, as a voice crying in the wilderness.

Keith S. Hodges

# INTRODUCTION

The young man up in Nazareth, along with many others, was hearing about the man preaching down in the wilderness, at the opposite end of the country. To say that wilderness preacher was unconventional would be a huge understatement. His synagogue was the open sky, rugged terrain, and a muddy little river. The young man, while working and taking care of his mother, had known for a long time he would have to go and have a brief encounter with the wilderness preacher. That awareness was just another part of an inner voice that had been preparing him for his purpose on earth for as long as he could remember. And now he knew it was time to go.

He'd left home yesterday, walking briskly in the warm and dusty fall air. But it wasn't as dry and dusty as where he was heading. It would be roughly a 60 mile walk, on simple roads and great highways, until he got to the deserted place he was headed. There he'd find a simple path, recently carved through the landscape by those going and returning from being with the preacher.

His mother had insisted he take some goat's milk, bread, and dried fish, which would be long gone before he would get there. Many others would have gone out of the way to avoid going through Samaria, trying to avoid contact with that region's despised residents. The young man didn't seem to mind. Instead he acknowledged them on the roads and as he passed through their villages. Sometimes those greetings were returned; often they were not. These roadways were notorious for the thieves who often took advantage of those traveling alone, beating and robbing them, and leaving them for dead. The young man was undaunted. He looked fit, as if he could take care of himself in any situation, and didn't look like he had a lot to steal. He slept along the road at the edge of a village. He'd be sleeping outside a lot for the next several weeks, and then a good bit after that.

He could have detoured slightly into Jerusalem, the biggest city he'd ever visited. He had been there many times for brief visits associated with the various feast days. He loved going to the Temple. He remembered fondly one time in particular when he was 12, and some fascinating things that had happened. His stepdad had died a few years ago—the man who taught him his trade, but more importantly so much about faith and life. The young man had continued to visit Jerusalem with his mother and younger siblings. He wiped a few tears from his eyes and walked on. Or he could have turned the other way and gone a few miles to Bethlehem, the sleepy little town where he'd been born about thirty years earlier. But not today; he walked on to the appointment he knew he had to keep.

The closer he got to where the wilderness preacher was ministering, the heavier the traffic grew. Most was on foot, some in carts, and a few on horses or donkeys. Though everyone was getting there as fast as they could, they all had time to catch a happy word or two from those returning, hearing about what had just happened to them.

The young man began to get excited about what his meeting with the wilderness preacher would be like. Those thoughts kept him smiling and joyfully reciting Scriptures he'd memorized. He knew this moment would propel him into a myriad of moments that would fulfill his purpose. He kept walking southward.

As he and others approached where the preacher was, a strange and wonderful scene began to unfold. Several hundred yards from their destination they started hearing a voice, indiscernible at first, but growing clearer and louder with every step. It was at the Jordan River, not far from where it emptied into the Dead Sea. The combination of water and the gentle slope down to the river made a kind of natural amphitheater, so the voice of one crying out in that wilderness place could now be easily understood.

There was a constant line of people waiting to have a brief encounter with the wilderness preacher. The young man waited his turn in the line. Off to one side were those who had just had their few moments with the wilderness preacher. They were milling about, happily discussing it among themselves. After a while they'd look over the scene, wave at the wilderness preacher if they could catch his eye, and start their journey homeward. There were others who didn't leave, but seemed to be helpers to the wilderness preacher. While the young man was waiting in line some of them brought the preacher a quick meal made from things found right there in the wilderness.

The preacher was standing waist deep in the water. He was giving short bits of a sermon, interrupted regularly by another person coming to him in the water. The technical term for what would happen with each person was baptizing. Actually it was just a simple full immersion of them into the muddy waters, made muddier by the traffic in and out at the river. The wilderness preacher would ask each person, in a quieter voice, if they were ready to change towards God. When they would say yes, he'd quickly plunge them beneath, give them a loving smile, and then look to the next person.

The wilderness preacher's voice rang out with the short but powerful exclamations about changing one's heart and actions from their sinful ways to the ways of the Lord. He was blunt. He spoke directly to different groups— the religious leaders, tax collectors, soldiers and others—about their need to change. The word he kept using was "repent." The wilderness preacher's voice was strong and passionate. As the young man drew nearer to his time in the water with the wilderness preacher, he appreciated as the others did the wilderness preacher's kind face, and his eyes that showed concern and hope.

It's not like the young man and the wilderness preacher hadn't met before—it was just in a different way now. Their mothers were relatives and had spent time together when they were both pregnant with these two boys. No doubt there had been playtime ("cousin time" is a special part of growing up) at subsequent visits and family reunions. So they were close to the same age, and bore enough physical resemblance that later their identities would be confused. They both knew this meeting would happen and what would come of it. When the young man saw the wilderness preacher, though not surprised, he was struck by his appearance. The wilderness preacher had long hair and a long beard. His clothing was obviously garnered directly from the wilderness.

Then the moment came when it was the young man's turn. He went to the man in the water. The wilderness preacher recognized him, if not physically then at some deeper spiritual level. The wilderness preacher was accustomed to spending all day going through his preaching and baptizing dozens upon dozens of people. But he realized this baptism was going to be different. He expressed his unworthiness to the young man, saying it was the young man who should baptize him. But the young man insisted, saying this is what he had to do to fulfill what his life was about.

John, the wilderness preacher baptized Jesus, the young man. But unlike with the others, John followed Jesus out of the water.

Suddenly something totally unique began to happen. It was as if the skies were torn open and something began to descend where they were. This dove-shaped Spirit went directly to and then into Jesus. Jesus immediately recognized who this Spirit was, like a reunion of closest family. He also knew this was as an even greater enhancement and empowerment of the inner voice to which he'd been listening for so long. John was ecstatic, as he'd been forewarned this would happen.

Then something even more spectacular happened. God Himself spoke. "This is my beloved Son, in whom I am well pleased." Others may or may not have heard it, but these two certainly did!

No other words were spoken. They knew they'd see each other again. Jesus began to move away, but not in the direction of the others who had been baptized. He wasn't going home; he was going deeper into what's called the "wilderness of Judea," the barren wasteland that lay alongside the Dead Sea. He took no food or water with him.

As Jesus reached the crest of a hill he looked back at where he'd just been, seeing that another person had moved to John in the water to be baptized. John also glanced at him. And then they both went on with what they had to do. John's ministry was not over. Jesus' would soon be starting.

The chapters that follow will examine the Scriptures that involve John, the wilderness preacher, and how his ministry related to Jesus, the young man. Hopefully these same chapters will help all of us as we try to fulfill our purpose in God's plan.

NOTE: This is a dramatization of events leading up to the start of Jesus' ministry, which included interaction with John the Baptist. It is based on biblical accounts. Some of it is hopefully reasonable conjecture of how things might have transpired. For example: (1) The Bible doesn't say when Joseph, the husband of Mary and Jesus' stepfather, died. But since there's no mention of him after Jesus was twelve years old, many believe he died before Jesus launched His ministry; (2) Neither does the Bible give us exact details of procedures surrounding the many baptisms John was doing, but hopefully what's portrayed here catches the feel of how things could have been.

# 1

## FRONT MAN

> "Behold, I send my messenger to prepare the way before me, and the Lord whom you seek will suddenly come to his temple; the messenger of the covenant in whom you delight, behold, he is coming, says the Lord of hosts." (Mal. 3:1; see also Mark 1:2b)

The old circuses which used to cross this land, making stops in cities, towns, and villages, often had a "front man." This person filled an invaluable role, and had to have an attention getting message. This was often complimented by being unusually dressed, often in very striking or loud clothing. This person's job, traveling ahead of the circus by a week or two, was to whip the town into a state of excitement, simply because "the circus is coming!" Not only did he hand out or nail flyers everywhere he could, he'd engage anyone he could—but especially the children—in alluring tales of all they would soon see, if they just went to the circus!

As crucial as it was, the "front man's" role was often a lonely one. He had to travel by himself, not with the camaraderie of all those in the troupe who would soon follow his trail. While he was always talking to people, only he, at least initially, knew his mission and the wonders of which he was foretelling. Oh occasionally, by some fluke in the schedule he might end up being in a town at the same time the circus was there performing. But even then, he was something of a stranger to the "circus folks." Certainly all of them, and especially the owner of the circus appreciated his efforts, for that's what largely made it possible for them to have an audience for each performance. But all in all, his was largely a lonely and thankless task. To say the least, he had to be a man of rather unique talents and temperament. You sure hope that somehow he got well rewarded for his efforts.

I'm guessing it didn't take you long to see where all of that was going!

John the Baptist's ministry was an indispensable part of the launch and success of Jesus' ministry. The several prophecies alone decry its importance. Oh, it's not to say that without the brief work of John there's no way Jesus could have started or succeeded. But in terms of the absolute, eternal stakes of Jesus' mission, the practicality and wisdom of such a strategy shines clearly. Why not do everything possible to give Jesus' ministry a running start? Or to use other metaphors, John seems to have been the last of many "prophets" to have plowed the ground and sown the seed for the ministry of the Messiah.

It would be an understatement to say that what remained of the Jewish people, a true "remnant," were eagerly awaiting someone special to be sent from the Lord. From a spiritual standpoint, they could reach all the way back to the Garden of Eden. There Eve (her name means "mother of all living") was promised that through her "seed" one would come who would "strike the head" of the serpent, that is the evil one. From that point on, subtly at first but then with a growing crescendo, prophesies upon prophesies built an expectation and longing for this "anointed one" (the meaning of "Messiah" in Hebrew and "Christ" in Greek).

So in God's infinite wisdom he planned and then sent, as it were,

His own "front man" to prepare the way for the mission of this Messiah, His own Son. We'll soon see the wonders of this forerunner's birth, upbringing, and ministry—all a part of the majesty and scope of God's wonderful plan of salvation.

# 2

## RUGGED INDIVIDUALISM

*John the baptizer appeared in the wilderness, preaching a baptism of repentance for the forgiveness of sins. And there went out to him all the country of Judea, and all the people of Jerusalem; and they were baptized by him in the river Jordan, confessing their sins. Now John was clothed with camel's hair, and had a leather girdle around his waist, and ate locusts and wild honey. (Mark 1:4-6)*

Of all the things one can say about John the Baptist, high on that list would have to be how he modeled rugged individualism. As we'll see repeatedly, his ruggedness was demonstrated in everything from his lifestyle to his dogged determination to be true to his calling. His individualism will show itself, not only in that "be faithful unto death" attitude, but in the fact that apparently much of his life was spent in solitude. Though it may be waning now, for a long time in my county the trait of "rugged individualism" has been admired, encouraged, imitated, but regrettably too seldom achieved. Hopefully our study of John the Baptist will give us a real refresher course in it!

[NOTE: For the sake of time and convenience we shall henceforth refer to this man simply as John. Later we'll distinguish him, as necessary, from John the Apostle.]

What's the first thing that comes to mind when you hear or read of John? It's probably his clothing or diet, and his ministry in the desert of first century Palestine.

You may have heard or read how "everyone's unique." But I'm sure most would also agree that some people are even more unique. We could debate whether or not there's any merit in trying to be unique. I contend trying to be unique is likely to produce a degree of fabrication that may come off to others as contrived or put on, because that's what it actually is. No, those who strike us and remain in our memories as unique, both to us personally and to our culture, are more likely those who are truly unique. They just are what they are. And if what they are happens also to be talented or inherently good, then their effect on others will be genuine and lasting. As an example, the entertainment industry produces a lot of seemingly unique characters who briefly make a big splash, but never really establish themselves as a star. They're what some now call wannabees.

I think instead of being wannabees like someone else, we should want to be what God made us to be. Our striving should be to make a contribution to the kingdom of God and our immediate culture, even if it's only in small and relatively unknown ways. But how we get to what we want to be can make all the difference. Will we try to do it by conforming to be like everybody else? Or will we try to let ourselves simply be the unique person God made us to be? Someone has wisely said that the best person you'll ever be is not trying to be someone else, but just being the best possible version of yourself. This is what John did so well. He seemed to be one of those who was "comfortable in his own skin." John's uniqueness in where he lived, how he dressed, what he ate, and how he conducted his ministry are really only manifestations of something much deeper in his soul—his desire to be nothing more or less than what God wanted him to be.

We're given information about John in the Old Testament prophecies about him, the unusual circumstances of his birth, and the lifestyle he chose. What we're not given are details into how the thought processes and decisions were achieved along his way. All we have is the finished product. It's obvious he made a lot of hard but good choices. Somewhere along the way he'd had to decide he wasn't going to live his life in conformity to any expected norms.

I've come to think of John's life as more than just a fascinating story or even an integral part of leading us into the ministry of Jesus. I think he is, in his own way, a good example for each of us as we achieve whatever degree of rugged individualism we can have for the Lord. Our successful completion of God's purpose for us being on this earth will have to traverse, no doubt, some of the same considerations John had. His story is in the Bible, in part, to help us be a man or woman sent from God.

# 3

## BACKGROUND

*And the Lord said to me ... "I will raise up for them a prophet like you from among their brethren; I will put my words in his mouth, and he shall speak them to all that I command him." (Deut, 18:17a, 18:18)*

*And this is the testimony of John, when the Jews sent priests and Levites from Jerusalem to ask him ... "Are you the prophet?" And he answered, "No." (John 1:19a, 21c)*

The first consideration many give to John the Baptist is when they see those early references to him in three out of the four gospel accounts. It's thrilling to trace the great impact of his life and ministry through those gospels, and then consider the references or allusions to him throughout the rest of the New Testament. But for our consideration let's go back to some very important prophecies concerning him from the Old Testament, lest we inadvertently rob ourselves of an even richer understanding of him and his role. Those Old Testament prophecies concerning him, by the way, can help clarify some possible misunderstandings about his identity and role as it relates to the work of Christ.

First, let's have a mini-study of the biblical dynamic of "type" and "antitype." (This can be a very comprehensive study and shed great light on the whole message of the Bible.) Basically this means a person, group, or principle from the Old Testament (type) is a reflection of a greater and more significant person, group, or principle in the New Testament (antitype). Prime examples of this would be: (1) Moses to Christ; (2) Israel to the church; (3) Elijah to John, etc.

So Moses' reference to another prophet coming is for most Bible students easy to identify as Jesus. At first glance we might be thinking we have an easily identifiable pattern with Moses as a "lawgiver" and Christ as the giver of a "new law" involving grace, life, the Spirit, etc. Likewise the great prophet Elijah could be seen as pointing the way (a "type") to some later prophet, who we will recognize as John. It gets a little more complicated (and potentially confusing), however, when we begin to see the use of the word "prophet" by Moses, as in the passage above. Then add a prophecy about Elijah as some kind of coming prophet. And then finally look at how the word prophet is used in connection with the ministries of both John and Jesus.

As we grow in our understanding of Moses' statements in Deuteronomy 18 concerning a coming prophet, it becomes clear he was speaking of Jesus, the Christ. (For additional references on this see John 1:25, 6:14, 7:40; Acts 3:22-23, 7:37.) So John was correct in answering he was not the Christ nor "the prophet." We'll discuss later how Jesus specifically referred to John as "the Elijah who was to come." For now let's choose to believe it was either in humility or innocent ignorance he also denied being Elijah.

Well then, what are we to make of Elijah, generally recognized as the greatest of the prophets (though he penned no Scriptures), and the connection between him and John? It's fascinating that when people started forming an opinion of Jesus (Matt. 16:14), they identified him both as John and Elijah. For that to have been true either John, who was killed sometime earlier, would have necessarily been raised from the dead, or Elijah would have had to have been somehow reincarnated in the person of John. This confusion, or perhaps just hypothesizing by people, really demonstrates how perplexed people were to the real identity of Jesus, since neither of those doctrines (resurrection or reincarnation) were widely held among most Jews at that time.

A crucial question for our early consideration: did John conduct his ministry out of some God-infused "instinct" (as if he were programmed to do it, and could hardly do anything else), or was his a strengthening that had come by what we might call the "hard way"—a steady and determined striving after God's will that spanned many years? This is important for all of us who want to be useful in God's work today. It's all too easy (and many do it) to look at others and say, "Well, they've been given every opportunity, and if I had been blessed with those gifts, I could serve God in a mighty way too!"

Admittedly John had been born into an exceptional family with some very "ordained" circumstances. And it's easy to infer at times that the Spirit had been active in his life for some time, delivering in one way or another vital messages about the work he was to do. But to answer the previous question ... I think John's achieving excellence in his ministry was a good combination of both giftedness from the Lord and disciplined effort on his part. It's really the same for us today, although not all of the details are the same. We should all remember that we have an advantage that neither the Jews before him nor John had. We have the completed gospel and the New Testament Scriptures. If we'll read them with the same eagerness and earnestness as if we were hearing the very voice of God, then we'll have "all we need for life and godliness" (2 Pet. 1:3). Then to that we are to give our own diligent efforts to apply what the Word is telling us (see 2 Pet. 1:5-11).

Hopefully you've come to believe (but like all of us need to be regularly reminded) that your being alive is not the result of a mere biological process, but ultimately as a part of God's plan. All of us will never have as monumental a task as did John, but our task, whether it be well-known or widely acclaimed or just some quiet service in the kingdom, is all a part of God's plan. And with that we need to trust God has given us exactly what we need in order to fulfill that plan.

John didn't just one day decide to go out into the wilderness and start ministering. He'd both been prepared (by God) and had been preparing himself for his task. And we have every reason to believe he continued that learning as long as he lived. We should do the same. As much as we can, we must appreciate the things God has already put into our lives to prepare us for our mission, while at the same time remaining open to continue learning from His Word and other Christ-servants how to fulfill our respective task better.

# 4

## JOHN IS ELIJAH?

*"Behold, I will send you Elijah the prophet before the great and terrible day of the Lord comes. And he will turn the hearts of fathers to their children and the hearts of children to their fathers, lest I come and smite the land with a curse." (Mal. 4:5)*

*As they went away, Jesus began to speak to the crowds concerning John: "What did you go out into the wilderness to behold? A reed shaken by the wind? Why then did you go out? To see a man dressed in soft raiment? Behold, those who wear soft raiment are in kings' houses. Why then did you go out? To see a prophet? Yes, I tell you, and more than a prophet." (Matt. 11:7-9)*

*And the disciples asked him, "Then why do the scribes say that first Elijah must come?" He replied, "Elijah does come, and his is to restore all things; but I tell you that Elijah has already come, and they did not know him, but did to him whatever they pleased. So also the Son of man will suffer at their hands." Then the disciples understood that he was speaking to them of John the Baptist. (Matt, 17:10-13)*

Anytime our Bible study brings us to a point where we need to start comparing passages for the sake of greater clarity, it can be both exciting and risky. Analogies, parables, and metaphors, especially when they relate to prophesies being fulfilled, can be great. The Bible's use of these literary devices is infinitely better than those we try to muster. But it's still tricky, in the sense that they can be, especially if we're not paying close attention, easily misunderstood or misapplied. There's probably no greater example of this than trying to fuse the prophecies about a "coming Elijah" and Jesus' words that John was that Elijah.

We've already looked at Moses' prophecy about another prophet like himself, but (by implication) even greater. This is clearly one of the Old Testament's many prophecies about Jesus and all He would be.

The prophecy above from Malachi was written after the Prophet Elijah had been transported away from earth, not having to experience physical death and burial (see 2 Kgs. 2). This promise is about him returning as a forerunner to the "great and terrible day of the Lord." As we'll come to see, John fulfilled this prophecy in his ministry which immediately preceded and slightly overlapped the ministry of Jesus. The exact meaning of the "great and terrible day of the Lord" is interpreted by some to mean the time and after effects of Jesus' coming to earth, or the gospel age, or the culmination of the gospel age in Jesus' second coming.

Unlike the Hebrew Bible, in our English Bibles (and many translations in other languages) the paragraph from Malachi cited above appears as the very last part of what we now call the Old Testament. Whether or not this was the intention of those who made this placement, Malachi seems to be the beginning of what some call a "gap" between the Testaments. Chronologically, there is about 450 years between when Malachi was written and the births of John and Jesus. It would then be about another fifty years before the earliest of the New Testament books would start being written.

So as it appears to us in the modern arrangement of Scripture, the

Old Testament ends with the mention of a "coming Elijah," and the New Testament opens with John figuring prominently in the story.

On several occasions Jesus spoke of the Scriptures (only the Old Testament at that time) with the general phrase, "The law and the prophets." This is, no doubt, why it was Moses (representative of the Law) and Elijah (representative of the prophets) who were summoned miraculously to join Jesus on the Mount of Transfiguration. But as important as these two were, God himself gave Jesus the preeminence by His declaration, "This is my Son ... listen to Him!" (Matt. 17:5).

Let me hasten to emphasize that John was not Elijah reincarnated. The Bible does not teach reincarnation. What it often does is use names symbolically or metaphorically, including the "type" and "antitype" we discussed earlier, to convey the significance of someone's identity or ministry.

In a later chapter we'll consider statements made by the angel Gabriel to Zechariah, who would become John's father. The angel said, "... he will go before him in the spirit and power of Elijah." So John was not literally Elijah; they were two separate people. John was, however, a person who could be readily compared to Elijah in the scope and power of Elijah's ministry.

EXTRA: While speaking of Malachi, there's a story I want to share—one of the funniest from my years as a preacher. We helped establish a new congregation in the Northeast. Early on we ran into a young man who had just recently become a Christian. He was very enthusiastic and evangelistic. As he and his wife, along with several they had helped convert, became a part of our congregation, they brought a whole new dimension to our fledgling church. Did I mention he was a second generation Italian-American? As a result of this association, many of the continuing number of new converts were young people—relatives and friends—who shared this Italian-American heritage. One Sunday morning at our worship assembly one of these new converts was assigned to read the Scripture; the first time he had ever done such a thing in a public worship setting. (We were so uncoordinated that we didn't think of assigning a reading to go along with the lesson. Each one could choose his own reading.) This new brother got up and said confidently, "I'm going to be reading from the prophet Me-laach-ee." (Say it nice and slow in your best Italian accent.) I sat there thinking, "What in the world?" Soon I recognized the reading as being from the book of Malachi. (I'd always heard it pronounced more like Mal-a-kye.) I could hardly wait until the service was over. I gingerly asked him why he had pronounced it as he did. He told me with a twinkle in his eye, "Sure, it was Me-laach-ee, the only Italian author in the Bible!"

# 5

## PREPARE THE WAY

*As it is written in the book of the words of Isaiah the prophet, "The voice of one crying in the wilderness: Prepare the way of the Lord, make his paths straight. Every valley shall be filled, and every mountain and hill shall be brought low, and the crooked shall be made straight, and the rough ways shall be made smooth; and all flesh shall see the salvation of God." (Luke 3:4-6; see also Isa. 40:3-5)*

At the end of our street in a small northeastern town was a substantial road named "The King's Highway." I had traveled on the road many times without realizing its most outstanding feature. Twenty miles from where we lived the highway runs through an even smaller town, settled in 1644 by European immigrants. The town's name reflects the heritage of those who established it. There's a story related to "The King's Highway," with some factual history and perhaps part legend. The governing British wanted to open a passable highway to the other end of the county. Apparently they hired a number of men from the immigrant town. The officials wanted to give the road a name that would honor the English monarchy. The immigrant workers had something else in the back of their minds. They were not building the road in honor of the English King, but in anticipation of a visit someday by the King of their native country—a visit which didn't occur until 1976!

Until it was pointed out to me, I had failed to notice the remarkable straightness and levelness of the highway. Unlike most roads then and now, there was extra care taken to eliminate the curves around natural barriers, the low places were filled in, and the high places were knocked down. Even in the 1980's, when we lived there, once noticed this bit of engineering was something of a marvel.

As stated, this story, at best, probably has a bit of whimsical legend to it. The story about John and his preparing the way for a coming King is fact, not legend. Notice again how John's mission as a "voice crying in the wilderness" had some of the same aspects as that highway in New Jersey. His daunting task was to be the immediate predecessor of the Christ. John's ministry was done exclusively among Jewish people. They had a religious heritage thousands of years in the making, with the last 1500 dominated by the Law of Moses. Nonetheless, there had been substantial drift in both their faithfulness and in their understanding of their role, as a nation of people, in God's overall plan. They needed their spiritual valleys filled, their religious high places (high-mindedness?) leveled, their crooked way straightened, and their rough places (laxity towards God's laws) smoothed. They needed someone to "prepare the way" for the ministry of Jesus as much or more as an otherwise unseemly terrain needs an easily passable highway.

In subsequent chapters we'll dig deeply into John's seemingly singular message of repentance as the essence of this preparing of the way for the Lord. But in the meantime, I wish to challenge you to do some thinking about various factors in your own life—from teaching you've heard to activities in which you've been involved—which in their own way have been a part of the necessary filling in, leveling, straightening, and smoothing needed in order for you to become a disciple of

Jesus Christ.

As you engage in this process, don't be afraid to consider things that might otherwise seem insignificant, almost childish, as a part of "preparing the way" for your own faith walk. Also, try to reach beyond the obvious "I grew up hearing the gospel." That certainly is an advantage in some ways and for some people. But at the same time we must realize that somehow that has failed miserably with many others. Far too many who have grown up in the church, at their first opportunity have bolted as far away from the faith as they possibly could. All Christian parents, church leaders, preachers, and teachers need to do all they can to not let the teaching and modeling our young people receive in any way be stale, routine, or devoid of passion and meaning.

Looking back on my own experience, I think two childhood and adolescent activities, totally unrecognized at the time as having future spiritual implications, contributed mightily. They were band and basketball. The former I sought. The latter was abruptly foisted upon me, with some resistance by me, simply because I was six feet tall at the start of 8th grade. One of the first and enduring things I learned in both disciplines is that you won't get very far having everything "your way." You've got to learn, practice, and perfect the basics. You've got to be coachable. And perhaps most importantly, you can't play (in those particular activities) by yourself; you're a part of a team.

Also notice briefly in this passage the phrase "the voice of one crying in the wilderness." This is what was prophesied of John in the Old Testament. It's how he chose to describe what he was doing. For a long time I merely thought of this in terms of his shouting his messages of repentance to the crowds. But more recently, perhaps as I've aged and witnessed how sin can ravage personal lives and society as a whole, I wonder if John's preaching had a certain lament in it, as if it was being shouted ... but through tears.

I'm from that generation that taught men they shouldn't cry. In the early stages of my ministry, I did everything I could to keep from showing undue emotion while preaching, for fear of being assumed to be soft. I had to get over that. Now, I often can't keep emotion out of my voice. I hope as we all get to know John better, we might have an expanded understanding of his being, "A voice, crying in the wilderness."

# 6

## JOY & GLADNESS

*But the angel said to him, "Do not be afraid Zechariah, for your prayer is heard, and your wife Elizabeth will bear you a son, and you shall call his name John, And you will have joy and gladness, and many will rejoice at his birth; for he will be great before the Lord, and he shall drink no wine nor strong drink, and he will be filled with the Holy Spirit, even from his mother's womb. And he will turn many of the sons of Israel to the Lord their God, and he will go before him in the Spirit and power of Elijah, and the disobedient to the wisdom of the just, to make ready for the Lord a people prepared." (Luke 1:13-17)*

Zechariah, a priest, and his wife Elizabeth, a "daughter of Aaron" (this means they were both from the tribe of Levi, the priestly tribe) were very godly people. But they were "advanced in years," well beyond the child-bearing years, and had no children. The beautiful story that unfolds in Luke 1 involving the promise, conception, and birth of John is miraculous, though not of the unique magnitude of Mary's virgin birth of Jesus. It reminds us of another aged couple, Abraham and

Sarah, who many centuries before had such a promise miraculously fulfilled in the birth of Isaac.

Please read Luke 1. You'll get the whole delightful panorama of John's beginning as a human, with some bonus material about the conception and pre-birth of Jesus. You'll also gain some great insights into John's parents.

God has good intentions for everyone. We'll consider this more as we move along. God has a purpose for every person's existence, or else they wouldn't be here. Everybody gets a clean start, and hopefully ends up with a successful conclusion. But in between lie three great areas with great potential for helping or hindering us fulfill our purpose. The first is our parents; the second is the friends and associates we choose; the third and most important are the decisions we make and the resolves we keep along the way.

Throughout this narrative Elizabeth shines like a jewel. She doesn't say a lot, but when she does, it's perfect. Most striking to me is how it mentions her being filled with the Holy Spirit. (That grabs my attention every time I see it in Scripture, because that's what I want.) Scripture makes it clear that God gives the Spirit to those who obey Him (Acts 5:32), that is to those who follow His commands and stand ready to serve Him.

We've already seen the angel telling Zechariah his son John would "be filled with Holy Spirit, even from his mother's womb." I choose to believe that's why John leaped in Elizabeth's womb at the sound of Mary's voice. Think about that for a moment. Here's one baby in a womb reacting to the presence of another baby in a different womb. John spent his whole life preparing and then serving the cause of this One for whom he leaped!

Zechariah may be the parent to whom most of us can better relate. Initially his heart was in the right place, but he dared to doubt the word of the Lord, delivered to him at that time by the angel Gabriel. The result was over nine months of muteness. How many of us spend periods of our lives, perhaps not as dramatically but nonetheless muted, because of our doubting God's clearly revealed Word?

Have you ever thought, perhaps with a little chuckle or two, about the difficulty Zechariah must have had when he went home and, without speech, tried to communicate all he had heard from the angel? I think those nine months were very sobering and productive for Zechariah. At John's circumcision when he was to be named, over the normal wishes of family and friends, Zechariah affirmed he was to be named "John." At the end of the chapter, himself also filled with the Holy Spirit, Zechariah prophesied about the life and ministry of his new son, among other things saying:

> *"And you, child will be called the prophet of the Most High; for you will go before the Lord to prepare his ways, to give knowledge of salvation to his people in the forgiveness of their sins, through the tender mercy of our God, when the day shall dawn upon us from on high to give light to those who sit in darkness and in the shadow of death, to guide our feet into the way of peace." (Luke 1:76-79)*

Wow! Way to go Zechariah; you not only correctly prophesied about your son, but also the mission and message of the Son of God whom he would serve. You, with God's help, redeemed yourself well!

# 7

## TALKED ABOUT

*And fear came upon all the neighbors. And all these things were talked about through all the hill country of Judea; and all who heard them laid them up in their hearts, saying, "What then will this child be?" For the hand of the Lord was with him. (Luke 1:65-66)*

The birth of a child produces talk! That talk can range from joy, relief, concern, and in some instances even scandal (like, unjustifiably, some did concerning the birth of Jesus). And while godly people give God the glory at the wonders of a child being born, you'll rarely hear talk like that which occurred around the birth of John.

First, notice the use of the word "fear." This is not because these events frightened these folks. Rather, it's used in the way the phrase "fear of the Lord" is used throughout the Bible, indicating awesome respect and wonder at the power and mercy of God.

Notice how some who heard of these things, "laid them up in their hearts." This reminds us of what's said about Mary in Luke 2, as she "treasures" or "keeps" in her heart all that had happened (so far!) with Jesus. What any of us treasure or keep in our hearts will make a big difference how we live as we go on.

Delightfully, we see the neighbors asking or exclaiming, "What then will this child be?" When I first noticed this line of Scripture years ago it made quite an impression on me. I'll tell you why. Much had transpired with Zechariah, John's father, and his experience at the Temple and subsequent muteness. Then came the late in life pregnancy, followed by the prophecy Zechariah made about his newborn son. But we must remember that John's birth story is not the only one in the Bible that clearly shows such providence and blessing by God. Moses' birth was like that, as was Samuel's. We can glean the same things from Jeremiah's conversation with God at the time he was called as a prophet. But without doubt it was the announcements, conception, and birth of Jesus that is the foremost of all of these.

The point has already been made and will continue to be made in this book, that while the particulars of the births and lives of most, including hopefully us, are generally not as spectacular as John's or any of these others, they are nonetheless important to God. With that in mind, we can join the chorus of wonder and awe and great expectations every time a child is born into a godly family, whether they be ours directly or someone else's. This behooves all Christians to notice, delight in, encourage, and help train as much as we can these children. And at the same time, we should be equally eager to do as much of the same as we can for those not born into the households of the faithful. God has plans for them too. Think of Rahab, Ruth, and all those Gentiles whose conversions we read about in Acts. None of these could have imagined they would someday figure powerfully in God's purposes.

This section about the beginning of John's life on earth ends, quite appropriately, with the line, "For the hand of the Lord was with him." Again, this must have been obvious to the people in that area, from the reactions we see them having just to his birth. Wonder what some of them thought thirty or so years later!

Let's think about what it means to have the Lord's hand with us—not only as it affected John's life but ours as well. These words can remind us of similar language in the 23rd Psalm, the Lord's Prayer, and "The Prayer of Jabez" (1 Chron. 4:10). From wherever you are and whatever you know about God, would you rather be living with His blessings and help, or without? I am always deeply saddened when I hear people say, "I don't want God in my life anymore!" Regretting whatever hurt or disappointment or misunderstanding has brought them to that point, I pray they will somehow come to think differently before their life ends. From what I've learned in my life, the thought of trying to live joyfully and productively without the Lord's hand being with me is a chilling thought.

Can't you just imagine that as John was growing up he frequently heard all the family stories about the circumstances surrounding his birth? At some point it seems most children ask about those things. It's not hard to imagine how John came to be so faithful. Not only was he learning the Scriptures, to love and worship God at home and at the Synagogue, but the very stories of how he came to this earth were being knitted into the fabric of his own identity. Christian parents today should do no less. Aside from little league sports and music lessons, away from the TV and computers, godly parents should talk to their youngsters about how they came to this earth and their family. Tell them the stories of how their parents met, and what challenges they may have faced to form a family. Especially if there were difficulties with the pregnancies or deliveries, let them learn to rejoice in their very existence. Whether the story is noble or not exactly perfect, the fact that this family is now on track to serving the living God—children need to hear all of that!

This final thought is purely speculative. Have you ever wondered what kind of temperament the little boy John might have had? Every child, by God's design, is to some degree unique in that way. I felt those differences the moment I first held each of our children in my hands.

So what might have the temperament of John been like? As one who may have spent a great deal of time in solitude, can you see John being one of those children who was content to play alone, and at times seemingly very contemplative about things? But then, as we'll see in coming chapters, there were times in his ministry where he was bold and outspoken. Do you think he might have been one of those children who didn't say much, but when he did it was with great passion? We don't have to know the answers to these questions to appreciate John. But especially in cases where we're not told, I oftentimes go ahead and assign my imagined personality or characteristics to a Bible figure. This somehow, for now, makes them seem a little more real to me. When we get to heaven if my imaginings were incorrect, they'll be instantly corrected, and it won't have mattered!

# 8

## IN THE WILDERNESS

*And the child grew and became strong in spirit, and he was in the wilderness till the day of his manifestation to Israel. (Luke 1:80)*

Maybe it's the kid in me, but I want to see the video! A wish I have is that when we get to Heaven, we'll get to see replays of all the Bible stories. That would be thrilling in its own right, but it will also answer many questions about all we're not told ... in passages like this one. I absolutely trust that the Holy Spirit and the inspired writers have given us all we need. But do you, like me, read passages like this and want to know more? When we get to Heaven, we'll be given everything we need to know that can be known. But I can dream, can't I?

We're not told John's age when he left the nurture and admonition of Zechariah and Elizabeth to go into the wilderness. Would it have been at thirteen, when Jewish boys were considered to have become men? Or would it be at twenty, another milestone of maturity, when young Jewish men were subject to the Temple tax? Or was it even later?

I'm more inclined to think of an earlier age instead of one closer to that time "of his manifestation to Israel." I have no reason to believe he didn't grow up as a young boy in the typical fashion of all Jewish boys, especially those in the lineage of the Levites. Jewish homes were usually strict in their discipline, training in responsibilities, and in hearing, reading, and memorizing large portions of Scripture.

The angel Gabriel told John's father (Luke 1:15) that his son was not to imbibe of any wine or strong drink. This could well mean he was raised under the "Nazarite Vow," which also included not cutting one's hair and other restrictions. This vow was usually taken by choice by a young man as a sign of his dedication to the Lord and separation from worldliness. In the case of Samson, and at least in part towards John, these stipulations were chosen by God for these individuals before their births.

I have wondered since Elizabeth and Mary were close enough to enjoy each other's company during their pregnancies, could that relationship and togetherness continued into the childhoods and youth of their boys? Can you imagine the little tykes John and Jesus playing together, neither of them realizing how intertwined their lives would later become? We'll see that somehow Jesus knew to go to John to be baptized. We'll also see John humbly trying to defer to Jesus on that occasion. But as to how and when these two gained those perspectives, we're given no clue.

I have wondered since John's parents were aged, if their deaths may have occurred earlier than most children have to experience. Could John have been driven, perhaps at what most would still consider a tender age into "the wilderness?"

We see examples of the "wilderness" in Scripture. Moses spent the forty middle years of his life there as a shepherd, being honed for shepherding God's people out of Egypt and towards the promised land. Freed from Egyptian slavery, the nation of Israel spent forty years wandering in the wilderness because of their lack of faith and disobedience to God. God taught Elijah incredible lessons in the wilderness.

Most famously Jesus spent forty days there, fasting and being tempted in the wilderness—perhaps in the same area where John had lived and ministered.

If you consider some of the spiritual and emotional implications, it gets easier to start to think of "the wilderness" as being as much of an experience as an actual place. Maybe you, like I, have wandered through several wildernesses of your own. "Wilderness" seems to be a real character building experience, especially if it is spent in solitude. Beyond human teachers, which are so important, I consider the great non-human teachers of spiritual strength to be one's personal use of the Word, prayer, service, and solitude. However long it was, and whatever part of it may have been spent alone, for John the facts of his acquiring spiritual strength and being "in the desert" is mentioned in the same sentence.

SPECIAL NOTE: The only aspect of John which some know has to do with his garments and diet – both of which are completely consistent of someone who had acclimated themselves to living in the wilderness. Locusts! Did he really eat bugs? Maybe; I've heard they are a good source of protein. There is also in that region the Locust Tree which produces a pod similar to what many of us would call a butterbean. Whether bugs or beans, he survived on it. His spirit had been forged in the wilderness, and he wasn't pretending to be something he wasn't. His uniqueness in these regards may have been the first things people noticed, but it's not why they listened to him, committed to change, and were baptized.

Before we leave the idea of "wilderness," let's consider some more potentially life-changing dynamics of it. The children of Israel, going from Egyptian bondage to the promised land passed through a section of Sinai named "The Wilderness of Sin." Ironically, it was there they demonstrated some of their fiercest doubt and rebellion towards God. Hopefully we can be honest to admit that all of us, whether for periods that were short or extended, have spent time in "the wilderness of sin."

The sad truth is that most who wander into that wilderness stay there. But that doesn't have to be! With God's mercy and providence, if we'll recognize and utilize the blessings He's giving us, we can be among the faithful who come out to serve God.

There's also the type of "wilderness" where we go for spiritual renewal or preparation. Sometimes God, in His own special way, leads (or even drives) us to this whether we're seeking it or not. Thank you, Lord. At other times we choose this because, frankly, we realize we desperately need it. In either case, it can be so helpful.

Wilderness experiences can be a make or break proposition. But don't be afraid of the wilderness if God takes you there. God brings good things out of the wilderness.

# 9

## A MAN SENT FROM GOD

*There was a man sent from God, whose name was John. He came for testimony, to bear witness to the light, that all might believe through him. He was not the light, but came to bear witness to the light. (John 1:6-8)*

The first amazing thing about the passage above is the simple statement, "There was a man sent from God." Depending on where any of us are in our faith and understanding, such a statement could prompt a whole range of questions. "Oh, how is this one different from the others sent from God?" "What, you mean people are sent from God?" "Wonder what God sent him to do?"

Some don't believe God (the God, a god, any god) had anything to do with us being here. We're just the current product of a long and complicated and mathematically improbable series of chances. Others have what is generally known as the deist outlook. They think God created everything and then left it to run itself—kind of like winding a clock and coming back to it sometime later before it runs down. These people would say we're only from God in the sense that He put the reproductive process in the first humans, that has continued, and here we are. Those first two views convey the ideas that either no creative type god exists, or at best that God is very impersonal.

I and most who call themselves Christians are theists, believing in a personal God who not only made everything, but is aware and concerned about us individually. An even more focused aspect of this theism is that God is involved in each person's life to the extent that He has a purpose and plans for one's life, or they wouldn't exist. Whenever I teach a teenage Bible class, it doesn't take me long to get around to saying, "You are not an accident, even if your parents thought you were!" (That usually gets a few giggles, but then you can almost see the wheels turning.) I'll continue with, "No. Your parents may have planned your conception and birth, or it may have been a surprise to them. But your real existence—its purpose and meaning—is from no one less than God Himself." It takes most of us a while to fully absorb and then trust that point. But with continual study of the Word, it can become a deeply held belief.

Believing that God has a purpose for my being here, if held long and strongly enough, will force a sincere person to eventually ask, "Okay, then: what's His purpose for me? What am I supposed to be doing?" This all occurs in the process we generally call faith.

This understanding brings us to even deeper questions, especially when we read a statement like, "a man sent from God, whose name was John." Hopefully, by seeing the prophecies, it has become apparent God had been planning John's life and ministry for a long time. That planning may have reached back like the plans for Jesus, being made even before the Creation. To really stretch your thinking, consider the possibility of God having a purpose for you and me, even before time began. We need to accept that while our lives may not be as dramatic or as well-known as John's, God still has some specific things for us to do for Him while we're here. I'm comfortable with that. Are you?

Please allow me to use a personal example. I believe God wanted me to be a preacher, although it's something I never anticipated or wanted, and for some time resisted. In retrospect I can see any number of circumstances and developments in my life that have helped this happen. But what if you're not a preacher, a Christian writer, or someone who plays some prominent role in your local church? Does that mean you are any less of a part of God's overall plan; that you are here without having a purpose from Him? Not at all! There are people who played key roles in my becoming a preacher that themselves have never preached a sermon, nor filled some leadership role in a church. But I believe God had them there to have an effect on my life at just a certain time. I say again: everyone is here for a purpose—God's purpose! To discover that reality and then pursue living it can produce great joy, just short of the joy of salvation itself.

Accepting and believing that biblical heroes like John, and then us too, are here by God's intention and design is a monumental thing to achieve. But it's only the beginning. I can't help but wonder as John came to realize his being sent from God, with all of its implications, if it didn't press heavily upon his thinking. He surely had to be asking himself questions like, "Why me?" "Can I handle this responsibility?" "Couldn't someone else have handled this better?" (Does any of this sound familiar to the questions many Christians ask themselves today?)

What John was sent from God to do will hopefully become quite clear as we move through his story. But before we move along with this, let's begin to consider how John may have been feeling about a growing awareness he was sent from God. How did it affect him in his view of himself or his purpose in life?

Don't discount the possibility that as John was coming to realize how special he was, it could have gone to his head! There's a host of other Bible characters, greater and lesser, to whom that happened! The same thing can happen today, as perhaps you've regrettably seen. Someone obviously has great gifts in some area of ministry and seems to be having a great influence, until pride sets in. Instead of being a humble servant of the Lord, they get to acting more and more like a Prima Donna. We'll see more of John's incredible humility as we go into his story. In regard to that, may I suggest you start asking yourself this question: was John's humility something almost akin to a superpower he'd been given by the Lord, or was it forged on the anvil of spiritual work and trials? When you find the answer to that question regarding John, you'll have likely answered the same question for yourself.

# 10

## NOT THE LIGHT

*There was a man sent from God, whose name was John. He came for testimony, to bear witness to the light, that all might believe through him. He was not the light, but came to bear witness to the light. (John 1:6-8)*

John the Apostle wrote the New Testament book known as "The Gospel According to John," usually just referred to as "John." John the Apostle was a close associate of Jesus almost from the beginning of the Lord's ministry. He was not only designated as an apostle (a messenger, "one sent"), but was a part of what's come to be called the "inner circle" of apostles—Peter, James, and John—who were exclusively privileged to share some key moments in Jesus' ministry. From references in his account, some believe John the Apostle may have been Jesus' closest earthly friend.

John the Apostle, however, is not the same John as the one we're studying in this book, John the Baptist.

The gospel of John begins quite differently than the other three gospels, particularly the books of Matthew and Luke. In the book of

John, there's no mention of Jesus' physical ancestry, birth, or childhood. Rather, John the Apostle and gospel writer is focused on introducing Jesus to his readers as the eternal "Word" (logos, the message from God). The emphasis is on how God became flesh and lived among us for a while. The introduction of the book, eighteen verses commonly known as the "prologue," with one exception focuses primarily on introducing Jesus. The exception is to introduce John.

If one wasn't familiar with the whole story of Jesus' ministry, nor had read the other gospels, and hadn't yet seen this John frequently mentioned in the gospel of John, this mentioning of John in the prologue would seem a strange thing. It's not just to distinguish two men who had the same name, which can certainly be confusing to new Bible students. Rather, I think it's because of John's prominence in the story of Jesus. John the Apostle and writer seemingly feels compelled, as early as possible, to differentiate between John and Jesus.

In the verses immediately before the reading above, the writer has stated, "In Him (Jesus) was life, and the light was the light of men. The light shines in the darkness, and the darkness has not overcome it." (John 1:4-5) This is why we see the word "light" used three times in our text, as "the light" (Jesus) is distinguished from the one who "came to bear witness to the light" (John).

The words "light" and "darkness" are used throughout the Bible as metaphors for righteousness and evil. Many times in both testaments God Himself is spoken of in connection with light. Therefore it is not surprising that when God in the flesh, Jesus, came into the world, John the writer refers to Him repeatedly as "the light." Later Jesus would refer to Himself as "the light of the world," and several of his teachings continued the use of light and darkness to draw the distinctions between good and evil.

The point is made emphatically: John is not the light, but came to give testimony and be a witness to the light. If you think this is framing the whole discussion as something of a trial, you're right! Collectively, all four of the gospel accounts present Jesus' birth, treatment of people, miracles, teachings, and especially His resurrection from the dead as evidence intended to verify His and others' claims that He is the Son of God (see John 20:30-31).

While John was not the light, it becomes increasingly clear John lived a life enlightened by God's truth, of which he was a spokesman. He lived in the light of God's will as opposed to living in the darkness of sin and depravity. It might be best said that John, his life and ministry, reflected God's light rather than being the original source of it.

Every school-age child is taught that the moon which orbits the earth doesn't actually produce any light, but reflects the light of the sun. I'm fascinated there are a few nights each month when that reflection is so bright you could, as the old saying goes, "read the newspaper by the moonlight!" But at its outset the Bible talks about God creating two "great lights," the sun to rule the day, and the moon to rule the night. Does that mean the Bible is scientifically unsound in every way? Not at all. Then as now, in everyday speech we speak of things which both produce light and reflect light as "lights."

This all makes more sense when we consider the words of Jesus to His disciples, "You are the light of the world. Let your light so shine that others may see your good deeds and glorify your Father who is in Heaven" (Matt. 5:14, 16). There and elsewhere, Scripture affirms that Christians are to be light unto a sin-darkened world. It's not that Christians emanate this light out of their own goodness or power, but they are merely reflecting the light they have received from "the Father of Heavenly lights" (James 1:17), and by their relationship with Jesus, "the true light that enlightens every man" (John 1:9).

John let his light shine, though ever so shortly, in a beautifully bright way. And so should we!

# 11

## HE CAME PREACHING

*In those days came John the Baptist, preaching in the wilderness of Judea, "Repent, for the kingdom of heaven is at hand." (Matt. 3:1-2)*

*The word of God came to John the son of Zechariah in the wilderness; and he went into all the region about the Jordan, preaching a baptism of repentance for the forgiveness of sins. (Luke 3:2d-3)*

Shakespeare wrote, "What's in a name?" in his famous Romeo and Juliet. To those young sweethearts, the fact their family names meant longstanding animosity meant nothing to them. But for most of us, even beyond literal meanings of the words or family pride, names mean something. Like it or not people do respond, if they know us at all, to seeing or hearing our names. I'm sure you're like me in how you want people to think or feel when they hear our names. We want it to be positive, even appreciative, and not negative or resentful. We should all try to wear both our personal name and the name "Christian" in a way that is honorable.

John's name is an interesting study. In Bible times it meant "the grace or mercy of the Lord." (Wow—think of the implications!) In Scripture many Jewish men are also referred to by a phrase which includes their father's name. Most frequently, though, with our subject, just the one name "John" is used in Scripture. But interestingly, many times there's the descriptive phrase, "the Baptist," (or occasionally "the baptizer"). This is how he is most commonly referred to today, both in speaking or writing about him. That nickname obviously grew out of the fact of his baptizing multitudes of people.

It's ironic in a way that John was given the additional moniker of "the Baptist," instead of "the Preacher," for it seems it was his pointed and powerful preaching that prompted the many baptisms. Perhaps the reason he was designated as "the Baptist" is that no one else was baptizing like John at the time he started his ministry, at least not nearly to the extent he was. I have heard attempts to equate John's baptism with some forms of Jewish ceremonial washings, or even various rituals practiced by cult religions. But these connections seem random and vague. It is more probable that John's baptism was a precursor to Christian baptism, just as John himself was a precursor to Christ.

A famous and successful African-American evangelist from New York City was once asked by a young preacher, "How many points should a good sermon have in it?" The wise old man thought for a moment and wryly said, "Well, at least one!" I think he was right! At least it proved right for John. I had one Bible teacher who adamantly taught that a good sermon should have an introduction, three points, and then a conclusion. (That sounded more to me like the template for a high school English theme than a sermon.) I'd suggest most of the great preaching in the New Testament seldom if ever used that pattern. John's didn't for sure. Oh, we'll see him making explanatory points in some of his teaching, but he was, without doubt, a one subject preacher! And his one subject was repentance. We'll try to delve deeply into that spiritual truth later.

The passage above says John came preaching "in the wilderness of Judea." This was the southernmost province of the larger territory known as Palestine. Jerusalem was there, as well as Jesus' birthplace Bethlehem and other notable locations, especially from Old Testament stories. But "the wilderness," also called sometimes "the desert" or "deserted places" was surely a small strip of wasteland located west of where the Jordan River empties into the Dead Sea. This was considerably south of Jerusalem and, especially at that time, uninhabited. Later we'll see John relocating his place of baptizing farther north.

It's interesting how often people entirely miss or miss the implications of the phrase "a baptism of repentance for the forgiveness of sins." That wording is the same in Mark's account. Jesus used the same words, "for the forgiveness of sins," in reference to His blood of the New Covenant when instituting the Lord's Supper with His disciples (see Matt. 26:28). After Jesus' ministry on earth was concluded and the church was beginning, Peter used the same "for the forgiveness of sins" during his sermon on the Day of Pentecost. Ironically Peter mentioned repentance and baptism, just as John had stressed (see Acts 2:38). I suppose the reason people tend to consciously deny or not see John's baptism having anything to do with forgiveness is some deference to the idea of "salvation in Christ alone." Please remember that while all salvation is made possible through Christ's sacrifice, those who lived faithfully unto the Lord in all previous times are saved by that same sacrifice. This would have included what we might call the transitional phase of John's ministry, including the baptism he practiced. I have no reason but to take these words of Scripture at face value. John's baptism was for the forgiveness of sins.

This discussion usually prompts the immediate question, "Was it therefore necessary for those baptized by John to then again be baptized 'in the name of Jesus' or 'into Christ,' as the New Testament later teaches?" Good question! We'll address that directly when we get to some relevant passages concerning that, later in this book.

Finally, I'm always intrigued every time I see a statement like "the word of God came to" in this case John, but also others on occasion. Here's a prime example of when I want to know more. How did this happen? Was it in a dream, from an angel, by an audible voice, or just some spiritual stirring deep within him? I'm not doubting it came; I'm just curious as to how, and for how long it had been happening before John launched his ministry?

The word of God comes to me regularly, you know, and it can to you, as well. Oh, I don't receive any miraculous messages, as would have to have been the case with John and many others throughout Bible times. It simply happens every time I pick up a Bible and open my mind and heart to what God is saying through the written Scriptures. The miracle is how this Word has been preserved through the ages, and it's also something of a miracle that a knucklehead and sinner like me started paying attention to it!

# 12

## REPENT!

*In those days came John the Baptist, preaching in the wilderness of Judea, "Repent, for the kingdom of heaven is at hand." (Matt. 3:1-2)*

*John the baptizer appeared in the wilderness, preaching a baptism of repentance for the forgiveness of sins. (Mark 1:4)*

*(Rocky to his wife Adrian, early in Rocky IV) – "We can't change anything, Adrian. All we can do is just go with what we are."*

*(Rocky to Adrian, later in Rocky IV) – "I guess what I'm trying to say is, if I can change, and you can change, everybody can change."*

Rocky Balboa, a fictitious cultural hero, made quite a metamorphosis in the movie referenced above. I sincerely wish this could become the new credo for the society in which I live, and all others worldwide. "Everybody can change." Instead (and I don't know exactly how this happened) for many today their quick response to many of life's challenges is, "Don't blame me—that's just the way I am!" Or you might hear many saying, perhaps even in justification of some attitude or practice, "Don't judge me. This is the way God made me!"

For the record: God never designed anyone to sin. That is a choice everyone has made, some more than others, along the way. By all rights, God could justifiably say, "You blew it; you're done!" But God has this part of His nature that is incredibly merciful and forgiving. He wants to forgive those who recognize the error of their ways, and want to change. God didn't make us to sin, but he did make us with the capability of changing.

The word repent means "to change." Sadly many folks, including a lot of religiously oriented people don't fully understand that. If you don't believe me, just listen carefully to how many use the words repent or repentance in a way as to only imply, "I'm sorry for what I did." Sorrow for inappropriate or sinful actions is an absolutely necessary part of repentance. It's where repentance begins, but it's not where it's supposed to end.

> *"... your sorrow led you to repentance. For you became sorrowful as God intended ... Godly sorrow brings repentance and leads to salvation and leaves no regret, but worldly sorrow brings death." (2 Cor. 7:9b, 10 – NIV)*

When John used the word repentance, he wasn't creating a new word, or new concepts about what it really meant. Some form of the word appears frequently in the Old Testament. But like with a lot of what God has given as commands or examples, through time they've been ignored or watered down so as to give them a meaning far short of their original intention.

John came preaching a message of repentance. Something about him and the powerful words he spoke didn't just attract a few, but "multitudes" from the countryside and city. We would love to know how his ministry got started. Was it with a handful in one of the small hamlets scattered throughout Judea, and then the ministry migrated to the wilderness and Jordan? When we're introduced to him and his ministry, the people are flocking to him, having to go out of their way to hear him preach and then to be baptized by him. With a bit of hyperbole (enthusiastic exaggeration) the gospel writers used phrases like "all the country" and "all the people of Jerusalem" went out to him to listen and be baptized (see Mark 1:5). We'll learn later that "all" did not include some of the religious leaders and others who didn't want to listen or obey. Maybe they didn't think there was anything of which they needed or wanted to change. It is most likely that the references to "all" meant a huge amount of people, or people of every type. It's the same way we might excitedly say, "The whole town was at the football game," while knowing there were a few elsewhere!

When John preached his sermons on repentance, he wasn't always what we'd call tactful or polite. He called some of those coming out to be baptized "snakes." The message emphasized not just the need for change, but practical ways to do it (see Luke 3:7-18).

He asked rhetorical questions like, "Who warned you to flee from the wrath to come?" To them he exhorted to "bear fruits that befit (are worthy of) repentance."

He chided those who would appeal to their Jewish ancestry as if that alone was sufficient for their salvation. He proclaimed that "God's axe" is already beginning to chop, and the trees not "bearing fruit" (good works coming out of one's repentance) would be chopped down and thrown into the fire. The spiritual analogy is not hard to understand.

He taught life lessons on ethics and generosity to all the people, with special directives to tax collectors and soldiers who were prone to extort others.

His messages frequently included statements of how he was baptizing with water, but there was One who would baptize with the Holy

Spirit and fire.

He compared this coming One to a worker who works at the threshing floor. He will separate the wheat (the good) into the granary, while the chaff (the bad) will burn with unquenchable fire. Again, the spiritual implications are not hard to understand.

After what some would call a rant, there's a most amazing statement. "So, with many other exhortations, he preached good news to the people" (Luke 3:18). Wait a minute! You mean that calling out specific sins and compelling people to change their sinful ways is "good news?" That's going to be shocking to some today who think that non-confrontational and totally passive messages are the way to preach. John would say, "No, you're going to have to repent, which means you're going to have to change!"

# 13

## A SPECIAL BAPTISM

*Then Jesus came from Galilee to the Jordan to John, to be baptized by him. John would have prevented him, saying, "I need to be baptized by you, and do you come to me?" But Jesus answered him, "Let it be so now; for thus it is fitting for us to fulfill all righteousness." Then he consented. And when Jesus was baptized, he went up immediately from the water, and behold, the heavens were opened, and he saw the Spirit of God descending like a dove, and alighting on him; and lo, a voice from heaven saying, "This is my beloved Son, with whom I am well pleased." (Matt. 3:13-17)*

Although I've read it and heard it taught countless times, as I typed in the passage above I felt like my heart was soaring. Just to focus on each phrase and try to imagine this scene, to try to drink in all of its meanings ... well, it's made my day! Mark's and Luke's accounts are essentially the same, with Luke only adding that after He was baptized Jesus was praying as the descent of the Holy Spirit upon Him begins.

As practically everyone knows, Jesus was born in Bethlehem of Judea, the province in which John was now baptizing. After spending a brief time in Bethlehem and his parents taking him to the Temple in Jerusalem, an angel's warning prompts the young family to flee to Egypt for a period of time. They intended to return to Bethlehem. But with additional information, Joseph decided to take his wife and the child to Nazareth, the hometown of the young couple. Jesus grew up there, in the province of Galilee, with one and maybe more occasional visits to Jerusalem. It was also there in Galilee where Jesus would conduct most of His ministry, with only occasional visits to Jerusalem, other parts of Judea, and brief sojourns into adjoining areas.

Jesus came from Galilee to John in Judea, at the Jordan, to be baptized. We're not told how Jesus was brought to this decision. Nor are we told how John had come to think it was Jesus who should baptize him, and not the other way around. It's not that confusing though; since the Holy Spirit had already been working in both men's lives, they had been given sufficient insights so as to make these decisions.

I've heard the question asked, "Did Jesus have to be baptized?" The answer, by his own proclamation, is yes. Oh, we know that since he never sinned, he neither needed to repent or be baptized for the forgiveness of sins. His words "to fulfill all righteousness" is one of those concepts we'll never fully understand this side of Heaven. But as we come to know more and more about Jesus, I think we'll grow in our knowledge and appreciation of how much He saw Himself as an example of humility, obedience, and many other aspects of faith.

Jesus' submitting to baptism, though not for the same reasons any of us have, is still a powerful example unto the millions since who have been baptized in His name.

Also powerfully on display is the first of several evidences we'll see of the great humility of John. Prior to this event John had already said to his listeners, "After me comes he who is mightier than I, the thong of whose sandals I am not worthy to stoop down and untie." He is saying, in effect, I am not worthy to even be His servant. Just think: after all of the ways God has acted in John's life, from before his conception up to that moment, John didn't let these blessings go to his head. That's humility. We're never told of any sinful activity by John, but Scripture dictates he would have been one of those who have "sinned and fallen short of the glory of God" (Rom. 3:21).

In his humility and obedience, John agreed to baptize Jesus. Matthew and Mark's mention of Jesus coming up immediately from the water after His baptism tends to confirm this was an immersion, that which the Greek word *baptizo* implies.

The immediate descent of the Holy Spirit upon Jesus was indeed a greater endowment of the Spirit in His life than He'd ever had before. But it was also a great sign of confirmation to John as to how God was and would be involved in Jesus' ministry. Later we'll see John recounting this very event as God's proof, this one whom he had just baptized, was indeed "the Lamb of God."

The Word of God has been given to people in a variety of ways ranging from visions, dreams, direct inspiration to prophets, and miraculously gifted speakers, etc. Many of these have prompted the writing of the Word of God, which has been preserved and used by numerous generations. Jesus was God's "Word" (Greek word logos) in the flesh. But only three times in the New Testament do we ever see God the Father speaking to people in an audible voice. John was a witness to this dramatically happening on one of those occasions. (The other two occasions were on the Mount of Transfiguration and close to the end of Jesus' public ministry.)

This is speculation on my part, but I can't help but believe John's hearing God speak in this way was one of many confirmations he would need for all that lay ahead. When things got really bad for John, I trust he was able to recall moments like this from his past and translate that into strength for the moment. I think exactly the same thing is necessary for us. As great things, faith-building things, happen in our lives we need to notice them and store them (treasure them up) in our minds and hearts. For as sure as anything times will come, suddenly and unexpectedly, where we'll need lots of strength. It's great to have some in reserve.

# 14

## JOHN BEARING WITNESS!

*The next day he saw Jesus coming toward him, and said, "Behold the Lamb of God, who takes away the sin of the world! This is he of whom I said, 'After me comes a man who ranks before me, for he was before me.' I myself did not know him; but for this I came baptizing with water, that he might be revealed to Israel." And John bore witness, "I saw the Spirit descend as a dove from heaven, and it remained on him. I myself did not know him; but he who sent me to baptize with water said to me, 'He on whom you see the Spirit descend and remain, this is he who baptizes with the Holy Spirit.' And I have seen and have borne witness that this is the Son of God." (John 1:29-34)*

Other passages reveal that immediately after His baptism Jesus was "led" or "driven" into the wilderness by the Holy Spirit. By the time we come to this passage that forty day experience has transpired, and Jesus has made his way back to where John is ministering. This may indicate the geographic location where Jesus spent His forty days of fasting and temptation could have been the "Wilderness of Judea," located on the western side of the Dead Sea where it's thought John had spent time being prepared for his ministry.

Whatever prior lack of understanding or conviction John may have had about Jesus' identity and role is now completely gone. John is now attesting to Jesus' mission, the comparative rank of Jesus compared to himself, Jesus' longer existence than his own, and God's predicted and completed sign of Jesus' unique identity as none less than the Son of God.

The phrase "Lamb of God" is one of the most richly symbolic phrases in all of Scripture. Since lambs had long been the primary objects of sacrifice, the full significance of this designation takes on eternal implications. The words "lamb" or "lambs" occur dozens of times in the Bible, but the phrase "Lamb of God" is only used three times, all exclusively in reference to Jesus and all by John the Apostle and writer—twice here in this context and once in the book of Revelation.

With this statement of Jesus' true identity, John, whether he realizes it or not, is becoming something of a theologian and prophet. He is making the connection between Jesus and the original Passover lambs. It was the blood of those lambs on the Hebrews' doorposts by which God's people were spared the death of their firstborn while the Egyptians received that last and worst of the Ten Plagues. Later in the New Testament, the idea of Christ being "our Passover Lamb" will be fully developed. John's statement also identifies Jesus as the "lamb that is led to slaughter" from Isaiah 53, probably the most vivid of the Old Testament's prophecies concerning the Christ.

Ironically John's statement, recorded in John 1:29, is one of the most often misquoted verses from the Bible! Since so much is said in the New Testament about the forgiveness of sins being made possible by Jesus' sacrificial death, many inadvertently say this verse using the word "sins." But in this verse, both from the original language and every version I've ever seen, it comes to us as "sin," in the singular. Whereas the forgiveness of sins, all important, is talking about the removal of our many sins, this singular usage is talking about the power of sin and its consequences, something akin to an alien force that has invaded humanity. This power is impossible to defeat except through the power of this Lamb of God. John, quite prophetically, is joined exclusively later by the Apostle Paul in addressing sin as a detrimental power or force plaguing humanity. Do you remember one of the lines in the grand old hymn, "Rock of Ages?"

"Be of sin its double cure; cleanse me of its guilt and power."

Many today use the term "witnessing" to describe the sharing of their faith. While they can do this as they explain the meaning and blessings of the gospel as it has affected their lives, they are not witnessing in the same way John is doing here. He was an eye-witness. To give credence to the assertion he's just made about Jesus being the Lamb of God to whomever was standing near, he now attests to the spectacle of the very Spirit of God descending, alighting on (Matt. 3:16), and remaining on Jesus.

Together the four gospels give us a complete view of the life and ministry of Jesus. But each of them individually has a special emphasis within the larger picture. In the gospel of John, the Apostle and writer's main thrust is about Jesus being the Son of God. What an honor it is for John the Baptist to actually be the first in that book to be recorded as saying it.

# 15

## TRANSFERRING DISCIPLES

*The next day again John was standing with two of his disciples; and he looked at Jesus as he walked, and said, "Behold, the Lamb of God!" The two disciples heard him say this, and they followed Jesus." (John 1:35-37)*

The first revelation in this passage is that John had disciples. With him having spent so much time in the wilderness, presumably alone, we may not be as prone to see him as a "disciple maker" like we see later in Jesus. But from this point on in the story, references to John's disciples will occur regularly, and continue on well past his death.

In contrast to great amounts of information about Jesus' calling and training of His disciples, we're told nothing of how John came to have disciples. For example, if John's ministry of preaching and baptizing preceded Jesus' by somewhere between six months to a year, then how soon or for how long had some been considering themselves, or considered by John, to be his disciples? We're also left to wonder if they were disciples only to the extent that they listened to his preaching, or did he, as Jesus would do, spend extensive time with them in personal or small group training?

Normally, a disciple is more than just a student. Their relationship with their "master" goes beyond the modern concept of a mentor. While disciples are gleaning all they can from their master's teaching, they are also imitating the example they are seeing, and making a commitment to follow this person or their ways indefinitely.

While these aspects of discipleship were, no doubt, occurring to some degree between John and his disciples, the very nature of his ministry as a forerunner may have also changed in what sense they were disciples, as compared to the disciples Jesus would have. To what extent John may or may not have anticipated it, his ministry was going to be relatively short. In contrast, Jesus was going to be ushering in a kingdom that would last forever.

John's disciples may have, in fact, been more disciples of his teaching than his lifestyle. I am unaware of any accounts of people taking up or continuing in the wilderness lifestyle of John, including his clothing or diet. What we do see later are some who are still following certain aspects of John's teaching, particularly the baptism he taught.

The second key revelation is the attitude John had as his disciples started to become aware of Jesus. This was true not only on this occasion when Jesus walked by, but in the ongoing development of Jesus' ministry. It's not hard to suppose that as John understood his role as forerunner, he also knew that in time his whole ministry would, in effect, have to defer itself unto the ministry of Jesus. In other words, to whatever extent he was making disciples of some, at the same time he was preparing them to be handed up, as it were, to the Christ.

This is humility with a name and a face to it—John the Baptist! Just imagine what would have ensued if John had started to develop an ambitious or selfish sense of pride about his work. The very thing he was sent to do would have been compromised, and Jesus or someone else would have had to quell the misdirection.

If you read on from the verses above, you'll see two of John's disciples following Jesus, having a conversation with Him, and spending most of a day with the Lord. One of those who heard John identify Jesus as "the Lamb of God" was Andrew. Upon his return from his day with Jesus, Andrew immediately went and told his brother Simon exclaiming, "We have found the Messiah" (which means Christ). What's the significance, you say? When they met shortly thereafter, Jesus gave Simon a nickname by which he's been mostly referred to ever since—Peter. Later Peter and Andrew will be some of the first Jesus calls to be His disciples. One can't help but wonder if James and John, and possibly other early disciples whom Jesus called, may have also previously been disciples of John. Do we ever read about John having any jealousy or bitterness, any clinging to his disciples as they were becoming Jesus' disciples? Not a bit!

We should consider some thoughts not about John himself, but about how his disciples must have been feeling as they were being transferred, as it were, to another teacher. Think about all of the multitude of people who were coming out to hear John preach and then be baptized. Spiritually speaking, John was the greatest thing these throngs of people had ever seen! He had a fiery rhetoric, just as they imagined Elijah or one of the other great prophets from a bygone era had. John's messages cut to the core of their sinful attitudes. Those messages made them willing to change. They believed John's message that God would deal with them like dead trees that had been cut down, or the useless chaff left over from the wheat harvest—ready for the fire. John's ministry was prompting a revival among the Jewish people they hadn't experienced in centuries. But now some of his closest followers are leaving John and following this new Teacher, with John seemingly endorsing Him at every turn.

Some of John's disciples, surely the most mature, didn't hesitate to make this change. I'm sure some were reluctant. We're not told how many of John's listeners and disciples would eventually become devoted followers of Christ. I suspect it was a lot.

There's probably a lesson for consideration here for Christians today. Our spiritual lives are likely to have, in fact we want them to have, a series of new awakenings and new understandings. To think we got it all at our conversion would not only be naïve, but dangerous. The devil is looking for people who think they've arrived. Don't worry; there is not someone greater than Jesus coming, as the next step for us in our spiritual development. But we all have to guard about getting to a point in our spiritual growth where we're comfortable, we understand a lot, and we might even think we're ahead of others in some ways. It's called complacency. It's when you've come to a place in climbing your spiritual mountain, and you're suddenly content to make camp only part of the way to the top. You reason, "It's higher than I've been before, and the view is pretty good from here." We can use other metaphors: "cruising," "in a rut," "taking a break" (which usually gets extended), etc. It's a very dangerous thing to start following Jesus, but then pull up short somewhere along the way.

# 16

## CONTINUING FOR A WHILE

*After this Jesus and his disciples went into the land of Judea; there he remained with them and baptized. John was also baptizing at Aenon near Salim, because there was much water there; and people came and were baptized. For John had not yet been put in prison. (John 3:22-24)*

*Now when the Lord knew that the Pharisees had heard that Jesus was making and baptizing more disciples than John (although Jesus himself did not baptize, but only his disciples), he left Judea and departed again to Galilee. (John 4:1-3)*

    I don't know about you, but I sometimes jump to the wrong conclusions when I'm initially considering scriptural things. Or worse yet, I might question God's judgment as to why a certain thing happened as it did. Oh, many Biblical teachings are straightforward and plain. You read them once and they fully make sense. Others take a lot of considering and looking at related passages before they begin to be appreciated for what they're saying.

Left to me I would have had John immediately discontinue his ministry when Jesus began His. John could have quietly returned to a life of solitude in the wilderness. Or he could have been given some new role, something like an apostle or "special assistant," during Jesus' ministry and the early days of the church. As in all things, I'm figuring out it's not a good thing it was left to me!

More than a few days had passed since we saw John identifying Jesus as "the Lamb of God." In the meantime Jesus has been conducting what's referred to as "the Judean ministry" for several months. Much of the rest of His ministry would be done in Galilee, to the north, with only occasional visits to Jerusalem in Judea. Jesus has started performing miracles. This in part prompted the dramatic conversation we see earlier in John 3 between Jesus and Nicodemus, a ruler of the Jews. That conversation morphed into the great gospel passage with John 3:16 at its center. Now we see Jesus continuing there in Judea, spending time with His disciples, and baptizing.

If one is not familiar with the Scriptures many questions are raised when people first read and assume Jesus was Himself physically baptizing people. That impression is laid to rest just a few verses later when it tells us it was not Jesus who was doing the baptizing, but His disciples (see John 4:1-2). Think of the jealousy or pride that might have arisen later when people could say they were personally baptized by the Lord. It's not hard to understand His disciples were doing the baptizing at His direction, or by His authority. But in those early verses of John 4, we also see Jesus' ministry rapidly gaining momentum, while John's is declining. We'll soon be exploring the reasons and results of this significant shift.

Fully understood or not, at the end of John 3 and into chapter 4 we see the simultaneous ministries of Jesus and John. Hopefully we're all learning that God's work and especially God's timing do not need our understanding or approval to work! A key point in anyone's faith is when they genuinely start accepting the sovereignty of God. Understanding God's sovereignty means accepting that He has both the right to implement His will, and what He does will be right, even if it's not soon or readily seen.

God's timing is rarely, while it's being played out, appreciated for what it's worth. We, being the impatient creatures we generally are, want things to move more quickly and decisively. Just one example: who would have thought it would take 1,500 years to convince people that they can neither keep nor be ultimately saved by the Law? But that's how long God waited until, "in the fullness of time God sent forth his Son, born of woman, born under the law, to redeem those under the law, so that we might receive adoption as sons" (Gal. 4:4-5).

While God had first John and then His own Son preaching a message of repentance (change), He knows full well that if certain aspects of that change occur too quickly no one will be able to keep up. So there's a period of transition as John's ministry is shutting down while Jesus' work is rapidly increasing. They overlap. It's like a will being probated; it just takes a little while. In regard to John's ministry shutting down immediately, I've begun to see how my thoughts would have been wrong, and of course, God's were right.

We'll soon see John acknowledging this changeover, and his feelings about it. There will be several steps, the first of which was John's radical relocation of where he would do his baptizing. Whereas he'd been baptizing in a remote area to the south of Jerusalem and other Judean cities, he now relocates to another relatively remote area, Aenon near Salim to the north of Jerusalem. But this second location is considerably farther away from Jerusalem than the first. A coincidence? I think not. It says John was baptizing at that location along the Jordan, "because there was much water there," making it easier to immerse people. But one can't help but wonder if somehow this may have been God's way, with John's cooperation, of somewhat stepping aside to let Jesus' ministry flourish in the south while John's declines in the difficult to reach area near semi hostile Samaria.

We can't always definitively say, "This or that was so God's will could be done." But neither can we dismiss that God is always working to put things together for His will to be done, whether we realize it or not.

Of course most of us know, as this passage previews, there's a two-stage tragedy coming. That will be a part of God's timing that will abruptly discontinue John's ministry. If you don't know the story, stay tuned for some intriguing developments. If you do, then you are probably already preparing yourself emotionally to revisit undoubtedly the most difficult time in John's life.

# 17

## FROM A DIFFERENT VIEWPOINT

*Now a discussion arose between John's disciples and a Jew over purifying. And they came to John, and said to him, "Rabbi, he who was with you beyond the Jordan, to whom you bore witness, here he is, baptizing, and all are going to him." John answered, "No one can receive anything except what is given him from heaven. You yourselves bear me witness that I said, I am not the Christ, but I have been sent before him. He who has the bride is the bridegroom; the friend of the bridegroom, who stands and hears him, rejoices greatly at the bridegroom's voice; therefore this joy of mine is now full. He must increase, but I must decrease." (John 3:25-30)*

*He who comes from above is above all; he who is of the earth belongs to the earth, and of the earth he speaks; he who comes from heaven is above all. He bears witness to what he has seen and heard, yet no one receives his testimony; he who receives his testimony sets his seal to this, that God is true. For he whom God has sent utters the words of God, for it is not by measure that he gives the Spirit; the Father loves the Son, and has given all things into his hand. He who believes in the Son has eternal life; he who does not obey the Son shall not see life, but the wrath of God rests upon him. (John 3:31-36)*

Things have significantly changed since John baptized Jesus. John saw the Spirit descend upon Jesus. The Lord had returned from His wilderness experience, to twice be declared "the Lamb of God" by John. Now Jesus has launched His own ministry, and John has moved his theater of operations to north of Jerusalem. Perhaps most importantly, the scope and magnitude of Jesus' ministry has begun to surpass that of John's. [NOTE: Opinions differ, but I favor the interpretation that verses 31-36 are a continuation of a quote from John the Baptist, and not supplemental commentary by John the Apostle and writer.]

It's not surprising some were confused as to why there were two powerful spokesmen for God ministering at the same time. This prompts a question to some of John's disciples, who go to him for answers. The very way John's disciples approach John is more of a statement of their observations than a question. The points John makes in response are astounding, not only in their clarity, but especially in their humility.

First John acknowledges a truth that all who want to follow God should accept, especially in regards to whatever your ministry might be. You have what you have from God, and not of yourself.

John then uses a powerful set of metaphors, all rich in practical and theological meanings: the bride, the bridegroom, and the bridegroom's best friend (what we now call "the best man"). No matter how lovely or desirable the bride may be, the best man understands she is intended for the groom and not himself. (This all makes a lot more sense when later in the New Testament we see the church referred to as "the bride of Christ.") The faithful best man rejoices at his friend's taking a bride. In this John is deferring any claim that he should be the one to go on and someday be the head of the church.

Then we have not only John's definite statement of his position in relation to Jesus, but one of the most humble statements in the Bible: "He must increase, but I must decrease." This was not a concession speech. This is John boldly asserting what he's come to understand over a long period of time. As crucial as his work was to God's cause, he was not the Christ, but the forerunner for Him. This is a vivid portrayal of the attitude every Christian should have toward our Lord. It's the embodiment of Jesus' call regarding discipleship that one must first "deny self." It's a portent to Paul's later saying, "I have been crucified with Christ, nevertheless I live; yet not I, but Christ lives in me!"

John really exemplifies his role as a prophet (which also makes him, in effect, a theologian). He does it by this brilliant contrast of He who is from above (Jesus) compared to him who is from the earth (John). This powerful testimony by John about Jesus includes these important theological points, which hopefully all Christians will also understand in a practical way:

- He is above all (stated twice).
- He bears witness to what He has seen and heard (possibly referring to the glories of Heaven, or the eternal plan of the Godhead to redeem sinful mankind?).
- Yet (tragically) no one receives His testimony. [This can remind us of the sad truths expressed in John 1:10-11.]
- Those who receive Him attest to this truth—God is true!
- This One God has sent utters the very words of God.
- He gives the Spirit without measure.
- The Father loves the Son, and has given all things into His hand.

Verse 36 is one of the most overlooked or misunderstood verses in Scripture, initially because it is so often poorly translated. A few of our English versions correctly translate a key part of the verse with some use of the word "obey." Others detract from its real meaning with words like "not believing" or "rejecting." From the days of the Old Testament right up to the present, those claiming to follow God have tended to ignore or downplay the place of obedience in following God.

I believe the correct understanding of faith is "trust and obedience." (It's like that classic hymn we sing, "For there's no other way to be happy in Jesus, but to trust and obey!") If one says they're trusting God, but to some degree or another is reluctant or even refuses to obey, then how much are they really trusting? Even the book of Romans, which many call "the epistle of faith," puts a premium on a faith that is an obedient faith. This is evidenced in the introduction (Rom. 1:5) and the conclusion (Rom. 16:26), and what might be called the "literary middle" (Rom. 6:17, with reference to Rom. 6:3-5).

This combination of believing and obeying spoken here by John helps make sense of later New Testament references to the importance of "obeying the gospel."

# 18

# EVIL OUTDOING ITSELF

*But Herod the tetrarch, who had been reproved by him for Herodias, his brother's wife, and for all the evil things that Herod had done, added this to them all, that he shut up John in prison. (Luke 3:19-20)*

In reviewing the whole Bible story, it seems that often when God is making an infusion of righteousness into the world, there is a corresponding, though not as strong, infusion of evil. This may explain the greater activity of demons during the ministry of Jesus and the Apostles, who used divine or divinely-given power to expel and limit them. It may also explain the line of kings in Palestine named Herod, corresponding in history to the birth of Christ, the ministry of John, the ministry of Jesus, and events in the early church.

With reputations well-deserved, these kings, all related, displayed a level of pomposity and wickedness reminiscent of the series of wicked kings in ancient Israel, and what would occur intermittently later by the Roman Caesars. The Herods were arrogant, power hungry, murderous, and immoral. The audacity of their behavior is heightened in that they weren't really "kings" in the normal sense, but figureheads put in place by Rome, supposedly allowing the Jewish people to feel like they were being somewhat ruled by one of their own. But the joke is they weren't even Jewish! They were Idumaens, descendants of the Old Testament country of Edom, a Semitic people distantly related to the Jews, but in no way close to them culturally or religiously.

The first of these is generally known as Herod the Great. He's the one who was visited by the Magi (Wise Men) and who subsequently slaughtered many young boys trying to kill the "new king" who had been born. The succession continues with sons and grandsons we continue to see in reference to John, Jesus, and the early church.

The circumstances surrounding the imprisonment of John involved Herod Antipas, his wife Herodias who had been the first wife of his brother Herod II. The original couple had a daughter, Salome, who became the step-daughter of her uncle, and upon whom a crucial event in the story will turn. So as a backdrop to the events involving John, there's divorce, an in-family marriage, and what appears to possibly be a situation of lust towards a niece/step-daughter. Into this domestic mine field somehow wanders John, a preacher of righteousness. We're not given much detail, but it becomes apparent as introduced to us in the passage above and all subsequent passages that Herodias, the former sister-in-law now wife, is deeply embittered towards John.

What I'm about to relate is not in Scripture, but rather just a line or two of speculation I heard years ago in a sermon. I can't remember where it was or who was preaching, but it made an impact on my memory that has never left. The preacher was depicting the courage of John, who in the imaginary scene he was producing for us in his lesson has John standing outside the castle of Herod Antipas and Herodias, yelling loudly (with those "voice crying in the wilderness" leather lungs, no doubt), "You can't have her Herod—she's not yours—it's not right!" I suppose even the wicked have a threshold of criticism about their immorality they can't tolerate.

John's confronting a king about what he considered an adulterous situation is reminiscent of Nathan, a righteous prophet of long before who had dared to confront a powerful and supposedly righteous king, David, about his sins of adultery, and the murder of his mistress' husband. Nathan may have been more tactful, with his use of an analogy that broke through to David—but the risk to both of these confronters was the same. A couple of generations of music lovers in America have been taught you don't tug on Superman's cape, you don't spit in the wind, you don't pull the mask off the old Lone Ranger, and ... (in situations like this) you don't confront kings who can have you executed with little thought about their personal morality.

None of us are Nathan or John, and most of us don't interact with heads of state. But church leaders for sure, and often what might be called rank and file Christians see or know of situations of impropriety to which they could and should speak. I'd say for most of us, our personal relationship with the sinful person may largely dictate the need to intervene personally. But with those we know personally, whether family members or friends, too many are reluctant to say, "I'm concerned," or "Can we talk about this?" No, many take the positions of "Who am I to say anything?" or "It's not any of my business!" Again, if it's someone we know, care about deeply or love, we need to ask ourselves, "Am I more interested in protecting myself from resentment, or in trying to help this person who is dear to me?" John put it on the line with Herod and Herodias. It's who and what he was. Are you surprised, really?

Few of us will have to do the things these prophets had to do. Ours might just be revealing to a worldly crowd that we won't do a particular thing because we're a Christian. Or it might be asking someone to refrain from screaming obscenities in front of your children. Each of us will have to make what we will of John's actions and what was to come of it, while we ask ourselves, "Is it better to go through life at least trying to be an advocate of things good and right, or just to remain silent and let unrighteousness go unchallenged and unimpeded?"

Finally, I noticed something for the first time from the version quoted above, how of all the evil things Herod had done, he added to them all that he "shut up" John in prison. Now within its context, this is merely another way of saying he put him in prison, or had him incarcerated. For some reason those two words caught my attention and I thought of the usually not so nice slang use of "shut up," usually spoken rudely to get someone to stop talking. It occurred to me that the bitterness of Herodias and Herod's own indecisiveness really didn't shut John up in the way that term is often used. His message had already made an indelible mark on that culture. As we'll see in the next few lessons, even after his death his message continued to resonate loudly in that culture. Through the Scriptures the powerful testimony of life and words continue to speak loudly to ongoing generations of believers. Nice try Herod—you can't really "shut up" a prophet of God!

# 19

## FEAR THAT DOESN'T REPENT

> *For Herod had sent and seized John, and bound him in prison for the sake of Herodias, his brother Philip's wife; because he had married her. For John said to Herod, "It is not lawful for you to have your brother's wife." And Herodias had a grudge against him, and wanted to kill him. But she could not, for Herod feared John, knowing that he was a righteous and holy man, and kept him safe. When he heard him he was much perplexed; and yet he heard him gladly. (Mark 6:17-20)*

I'm fascinated how some seem to have a certain regard, perhaps even respect, not just for religious people in general but especially religious leaders, though they may have no actual interest in learning from them or ascribing to their beliefs. Some of this may just be political correctness, for it's often politicians or the media that is most obvious in doing this. Although there are more and more who don't seem to mind showing disrespect or even contempt for religious leaders, these public figures must deem it unwise to let it be seen. But then there are ordinary folks too who seem to be very reluctant to criticize or impugn the motives of religious folks or their leaders. Maybe in the back of their minds there's just a little bit of fear of "What if they're right?" and that attacking or offending them might bring repercussions they don't want.

In the case of John, the adulterous wife Herodias is just mad. She couldn't care less about what John believes or supposedly stands for. He's criticizing her privately, if not publicly, and she wants this new husband to off him, in this instance quite literally.

Herod, on the other hand, is handling this in a totally different way than her, but not that differently than the way a lot of people handle such matters. He was conflicted. Conflicted people are miserable people, and often have strange combinations of thoughts, attitudes, and actions. I know, for sometimes I am one of them. Thankfully not as much as I used to be, but I'm still human and it creeps up on me every now and then. I or anybody else can get un-conflicted, by the way, by getting back into the will of God and out of self-will.

The text says Herod feared John and considered him to be a righteous and holy man. Therefore he kept him safe. The use of the word "fear" may not be that dissimilar to the way it's used in the Bible in reference to fearing God. It's not just being afraid of consequences alone, but mixed with a healthy blend of respect. While Herod was probably catching constant grief from his wife, at the same time some significant part of him couldn't deny that John's life and ministry seemed to bear evidence of being more than just human effort. It's like a lot of people today. They'd like to deny God in their lives, and generally discount those who believe in Him, and they also find themselves reluctant to go ahead and accept the message. Something is holding them back. Ultimately it boils down to loving their own ways, sinful though they are, more than they love the idea of yielding to a higher authority, namely God. It's really a matter of pride. Am I going to live my life "God's way" or "my way?"

We're then told that Herod "heard him gladly," but at the same time was perplexed. Does that strike you as an odd combination? Recently we took one of our granddaughters to the circus. There were several of the acts that I enjoyed watching, like the high wire or flying trapeze, but I would never consider attempting them. We must remember that in much the same way many people can somehow be entertained, amused, or even awestruck by spiritual beliefs they would never consider having or following. There's a certain curiosity, but not enough to ever prompt joining the activity. I think all of us are so accustomed to being spectators in so many arenas—entertainment or sports—that can carry over into matters of faith. It's relatively easy to be one who endorses or is even a fan of religious activity, but not really be a full-fledged participant. The first time I heard this, just as a pre-teen, was when I heard someone say, "Oh we're (their religious affiliation), but not devout." Somehow God helped me remember isolated statements like that when I started seriously studying the Bible. I've never found in the Bible that just "belonging" to a church (in the usual sense of how that's spoken) is mentioned, but being devoted to the Lord and His ways is!

Herod, possibly for a variety of reasons like his family heritage, his ruling position, his wife's nagging, or his own inclination toward a sinful lifestyle, chose to listen to John and even let him disturb him a little, but not accept and obey. This pattern of human behavior is seen throughout the whole Bible. It surely is one of the reasons that many who are exposed to the gospel never believe it.

Finally, what if Herod had decided to believe John, repent, and let the wilderness preacher baptize him? He might have lost the wife he wasn't supposed to have had in the first place. He might have lost his role as Tetrarch (an unimportant king), he might have even lost his life. But he would have been saved. It's that "cost of discipleship" Jesus talked about during His ministry. It's a choice people make every day, one way or the other. How about you?

We'll return to this account from Mark's gospel of the imprisonment of John. But first let's explore some fascinating things that transpired during that imprisonment.

# 20

## WHY THIS QUESTION, NOW?

*Now when John heard in prison about the deeds of the Christ, he sent word by his disciples and said to him, "Are you he who is to come, or shall we look for another?" And Jesus answered them, "Go and tell John what you hear and see: the blind receive their sight and the lame walk, lepers are cleansed and the deaf hear, and the dead are raised up, and the poor have good news preached to them. And blessed is he who takes no offense at me." (Matt. 11:2-6)*

Imprisonment can do strange things to the minds of even the strongest of men. (Do any of you remember the warden in Cool Hand Luke who kept Luke and others in "the box" for thirty days to "get their mind right?") Incarceration not only keeps the dangerous criminals away from innocent people, but it can be a very sobering, even confusing, time for the one being punished. John, like Jesus who would follow him in receiving undue punishment, was not a criminal. His "offense" was for speaking a righteous truth to an unrighteous man and his, perhaps even more, unrighteous wife.

This passage comes with Jesus fully engaged in His ministry of teaching and performing miracles. We might be surprised to see that while John was imprisoned he could be visited by his disciples. Upon hearing of these great works of compassion and healing by Jesus, John had used the occasion to make what we have as his final appeal of the Lord. "Are you he who is to come, or shall we look for another?"

Jesus sends those disciples with a "tell John what you see and hear" message including healings of the blind, the lame, lepers, the deaf, and the dead being raised up. Luke's account has Jesus also mentioning evil spirits being cast out. But another simple part of the answer that's easy to overlook is when Jesus included the poor having the gospel preached to them. I suppose to some, anybody paying any real attention to the poor is as much of a miracle as all those healings. Then Jesus concludes his answer to John with these challenging words, "And blessed is he who takes no offense at me."

It's hard to imagine that one who had so valiantly been that "voice crying out in the wilderness," who had endured the harshness of the wilderness itself, and the interrogation of the religious leaders, that he could be having doubts about Jesus being the Christ. After all, he was the very one who upon two successive days had declared to his own disciples that Jesus, as He was passing by, was indeed "the Lamb of God." To validate this claim John attested to what he had seen with his own eyes, the Spirit of God descending in the manner of a dove, and alighting on Jesus. As a part of his declaration that Jesus was the Lamb of God, John explained he had been told to anticipate this, and it had happened just as he'd been told it would. But now John, with some passage of time, his unjustified arrest, and a period of imprisonment, was dispatching messengers to ask in effect, "Are you the one?"

I'll give John the benefit of the doubt in two ways. First, this question and the answer may not have been for John's benefit at all. It could have been another act of humility by which John was further releasing his disciples to become followers of Jesus. Maybe the loyalty of some of these disciples to John was so great, the only way he could get them to start following Jesus was for them to see and to hear for themselves. Then there's the possibility that John was being affected by his imprisonment. Maybe he was thinking "I'm going to rot away in this jail, or be put to death, and am I certain it's for the right cause?" Certain things, but especially the threat of imminent death, does tend to give us humans pause, to reflect on what our life has been about and if our course of action was the right one.

Quite unintentionally I was introduced in person to Lord Byron's "The Prisoner of Chillon," a long and epic poem depicting the plight of a man imprisoned as a part of the Reformation. I was a rather uneducated nineteen-year-old traveling through Europe on a tour bus, which stopped at a beautiful castle built out into Lake Geneva. In the next hour and a half my interest shifted from the beautiful lake, countryside, and castle to the story of a man who spent many years in its dungeon. His father and three of his brothers had died in battle or been tortured to death. Now he and his two remaining brothers were chained and slept on the dirt floor in the dungeon, actually below the surface of the lake. In time the two brothers died in their chains. The prisoner eventually broke free from his chains and spent his days wandering around the dungeon, being careful not to step where the bodies of his deceased brothers lay. At times the prisoner almost gave in to his own pity, being occasionally encouraged by the sound of a bird chirping outside, or the incredible view obtained with great difficulty. I myself was drawn to that little opening, and couldn't help but notice how the window sill below it had been hollowed out by many doing what I was about to do—hoist myself up for a quick but tiring look outside. The view was almost at the same level as the water, and across the way you could see the opposite shore, tall trees, and the majestic Alps in the distance. I could also sense a whiff of fresh air, compared to the mustiness you might expect in such a place. I was able to immediately empathize with the prisoner, and wondered what it would be like to spend a big portion of your life in such a place. It was only later I wondered if John had such harrowing days and nights, pacing back and forth in whatever area of confinement he occupied. And what floods of questions must have raced through his head. "Did I do all of that for God to end up like this?" John's plight, like Christ's sacrifice, and like the martyrdom of countless Christians through the centuries became more real to me because of my unexpected stop there in the Swiss countryside.

Who among us, at some dark and lonely part of our Christian journey hasn't had the same kind of questioning thoughts? Is this my reward for being faithful? Whatever reason John had for sending this question to Jesus, he obviously didn't "take offense" at Him. A lesser man might have said, "I'm outta here; I don't deserve this." He could have called for Herod and Herodias, apologized for his insulting remarks, promised he would never do that kind of preaching again, and slipped away in time and history. But that wasn't the essence of John, for he remained in prison, unyielding to any temptation to deny the Lord for whom he had prepared the way. May we be such people!

# 21

## NONE GREATER THAN JOHN

*As they went away, Jesus began to speak to the crowds concerning John: "What did you go out into the wilderness to behold? A reed shaken by the wind? Why then did you go out? To see a man clothed in soft raiment? Behold, those who wear soft raiment are in kings' houses. Why then did you go out? To see a prophet? Yes, I tell you, and more than a prophet. This is he of whom it is written, "Behold, I send my messenger before thy face, who shall prepare thy way before thee." Truly, I say to you, among those born of women there has risen no one greater than John the Baptist; yet he who is least in the kingdom of heaven is greater than he. From the days of John the Baptist until now the kingdom of heaven has suffered violence, and men of violence take it by force. For all the prophets and the law prophesied until John; and if you are willing to accept it, he is Elijah who is to come. He who has ears to hear, let him hear. But to what shall I compare this generation? It is like children sitting in the market places and calling to their playmates, "We piped to you, and you did not dance; we wailed, and you did not mourn." For John came neither eating nor drinking,*

> *and they say, "He has a demon"; the Son of man came eating and drinking, and they say, "Behold, a glutton and a drunkard, a friend of tax collectors and sinners!" Yet wisdom is justified by her deeds. (Matt. 11:7-19)*

After His hearing and answering the question sent from John by some of his disciples, Jesus uses the occasion to praise John, informing or reminding His hearers of some important elements of John's story:

- He was not "a reed shaken by the wind," probably attesting to his real strength as a person.
- He wasn't a preacher who drew attention to himself by fancy clothes, but just the opposite.
- He didn't afford himself any of the luxuries of royalty or prominence.
- He was not only a prophet, but the very one who had been prophesied to be a special messenger sent to prepare the way for the Lord.
- John didn't come drinking (remember his "Nazarite Vow" which allowed for no wine or strong drink) or eating (probably meaning rich and tasty foods, compared to living off the land in the wilderness).

Within this praise of John, the Lord then offered a line of Scripture that has been challenging Bible students ever since. He basically said John has a greatness about himself that surpasses all others who have ever lived. Think of all the Old Testament heroes that includes! But Jesus then makes the startling statement that whomever might be seen as the "least" (most unimportant) in the kingdom of God is greater than John.

Before delving into this fully, let me hasten to say that no serious Bible student should ever think that any person in the church, whether supposedly important or unimportant, surpasses John in his faith, the magnitude of his mission, or fortitude. While we've probably all heard of the incredible devotion and sacrifice of martyrs and saints down through the ages, the combination of humility and toughness seen in John was only surpassed by Jesus Himself, and not by any Christian I've known or heard about since. But Jesus said it. In some sense He was saying that whomever might seem to be an almost unnoticeable church member (one who is in the kingdom) has a certain greatness to him or her not accorded even to John. So let's try to figure out what Jesus was saying.

This whole discussion might remind us of Paul's instruction about honoring different parts of "the body" (members of the church) in 1 Corinthians 12. There in verses 24 and 25 Paul plainly states the greater honor should be given to the "lesser" or "inferior" parts of the body, and not the supposedly greater ones.

We must try to remember the crescendo of first John's and now Jesus' teaching about the kingdom of God. Both preachers declared it was "at hand," meaning its essence is very near. Within the passage cited above Jesus Himself declared that since the days of John the Baptist (that is, when John started his ministry), "the kingdom of heaven has been forcefully advancing, and forceful men lay hold of it" (Matt.11:12, NIV). In other words, to some degree kingdom power has already been at work, first in the ministry of John and now in Jesus' ministry as well. At the same time, we must remember the several times in which Jesus seems to speak clearly of the kingdom as not having "come" (see Matt. 6:10 and Luke 9:27). It's a whole different study, but the church Jesus had promised to build, and which was begun on the Day of Pentecost (Acts 2), seems to be the fulfillment of the kingdom on earth, as from that point on it is spoken of as existent.

From other passages we gain that being a part of this kingdom will not be based on one's physical birth, but by their rebirth—a commitment of faith to Jesus Christ and His gospel.

So the greatness of even "the least in the kingdom" is not a matter of recognized significance or accomplishment, but one of privilege. While John and all the faithful who lived before Christ will be in Heaven, every Christian (those in the kingdom of God on earth) is better equipped and positioned to work for God than all those faithful ones who came before. They'll have learned of the gospel as facts that have happened, and not just prospectively. Each one will have received the gift of the Holy Spirit. In their baptism, they've already participated in the resurrection of Christ and will witness the resurrection of all the faithful at Jesus' return. God had many wonderful people who lived and died in faith on the other side of the cross, the foremost of whom was John the Baptist. But those us who have lived "in Christ" on this side of the cross are even more privileged! May we never forget it!

# 22

## THE OPPORTUNITY FOR EVIL

> *But an opportunity came when Herod on his birthday gave a banquet for his courtiers and officers and the leading men of Galilee. For when Herodias' daughter came in and danced, she pleased Herod and his guests; and the king said to the girl, "Ask me for whatever you wish, and I will grant it." And he vowed to her, "Whatever you ask me, I will give you, even half of my kingdom." And she went out and told her mother, "What shall I ask?" And she said, "The head of John the baptizer." (Mark 6:21-24)*

Make no mistake about it, opportunities to do either good or bad, righteous things or evil things, will present themselves to everyone. The idea that unrighteousness will never present itself just because someone doesn't want to do evil is somewhere between naïve and reckless.

But there is an axiomatic truth regarding opportunities that come our way regarding good or evil. The number of opportunities on either side of that equation go up exponentially in response to the attitude one has, those with whom they associate, and where they spend their time. In other words, temptations towards evil things will come up even if you have no desire or intention for them to do so. But if your activities and associations are evil, those opportunities to do wrong will come at you more and faster than you can imagine. Conversely, when we're looking to do good, to serve righteousness instead of evil, more opportunities than we can ask or imagine will present themselves.

King Herod gave a birthday party for himself. I'm not anti-birthday celebrations. The actual births of people and things like the church (Acts 2) are given great honor and recognition in Scripture. It's just in this party at Herod's palace, and a similar one (not necessarily a birthday party) by King Ahasuerus (or Xerxes) in the book of Esther both appear to be nothing but self-indulgent spectacles that lent themselves to nothing good, at least in the moment.

Is there any reason to assume the party Herod was hosting was anything but a drunken bash of a bunch of successful men, with egos and possibly libidos, as we would say, off the charts? Add to this potential powder keg the dance of what we'd suppose is a young woman, possibly even a young teenage girl. If I were writing a novel about this and wanted to sensationalize it, I'd have her be about fifteen, but looking like she was eighteen or older. She would be scantily clad, and her dance (though the Bible doesn't specify this) would be as provocative and seductive as it could possibly be. (It's hard to imagine her in this setting being a ballerina, or doing a modest interpretive dance!) I could even add to my novel that Herod had already had his eye on his niece who is now living there as his stepdaughter. Again, the Bible doesn't suggest any of that, but we can't discount those and other possibilities.

But I'm not writing a novel. This is a true and tragic story. Something did happen as a result of Salome's dance. Possibly fueled by some combination of intoxication, infatuation or lust, and probably just some pure old showing off in front of his officials, Herod makes, as we'll soon see, what he recognizes later as some terribly ill-advised promises to Salome.

This episode turns out to be more of a lesson in how life works than we might notice at first glance. First consider the foolish offer by Herod. Was he merely drunk? Was he so lustful or at least infatuated towards the girl that he made an outlandish offer that he didn't think he would have to honor? People do make outlandish offers or boasts when they think they are being guided by "love," when really it's just self-serving lust or passion. All of this is speculative, a lot of reading between the lines by folks like us. The one thing of which I am quite certain is that Herod wasn't expecting Salome's request to be what it was. Oh, even when the request came if he'd been enough of a man he would have brought himself to say, "I'm sorry. That was a foolish thing for me to say. I will take the blame for it. But I cannot allow this man to be killed just because of my idle boast." He could have done that, if he'd been a big enough man.

Consider next the girl Salome. While somehow or other she allowed herself to be used in this provocative way, it doesn't seem she was fully complicit in some plan to use this occasion to get rid of John. As we're already doing, we could continue to have wild speculation about whatever the young woman thought she might gain from this activity. But somehow we get the feeling that without realizing the consequences that would come, she nonetheless allowed herself to be used in this way, maybe even enjoying it. Again a life lesson for us. When people participate in worldly things, they should not be all that surprised at what may come of it. But in such instances most people feign ignorance or innocence saying, "I had no idea this would happen." As we said before, when we put ourselves in wrong situations with the wrong people, we should never be surprised at some incredibly bad outcomes. But many are.

It's interesting that when Salome heard this offer from Herod, she didn't have a ready answer. Instead she went to her mother, the very one who most despised John. Another life lesson, when you're in trouble or doubt, be careful to whom you go for advice. If it's someone who helped put you in a precarious predicament, then you had better steer clear. Of course, with Herodias being Salome's mother, it seems logical the young woman would do that instead of just asking for something off the top of her head. Still this gave the unrighteous Herodias the very opportunity for which she had been longing—to be rid of that agonizing nuisance named John.

Once the girl returned with the request, weak Herod capitulated, and he ordered John executed. To show how macabre the situation was, instead of just knowing John's execution had occurred, John's head was brought back to the girl, at her mother's request, on a platter (like a hunter's trophy), and the girl took it to her mother. This reminds me of many stories I've heard of how evil people seem to take delight in watching the torture of their enemies. When people don't believe in eternity, judgment, the value of people, etc. there's no telling what they'll do!

# 23

## DEEP RESPECT

*Now when Jesus heard this, he withdrew from there in a boat to a lonely place apart. (Matt. 14:13)*

Those familiar with the gospel accounts soon pick up on the fact that during much of Jesus' ministry he tried, usually unsuccessfully, to get away at times with His disciples to teach them privately. So we might assume this was just another attempt to get away from those ever-pressing crowds, unless we pay close attention to this line in Matthew's account.

As indicated earlier, we don't know how much time in earlier years Jesus and John might have spent together, as cousins often do, first just playing together and then as they matured, sharing growing up thoughts together. We do know that Jesus has already demonstrated by His coming to John to be baptized, and then later by His comments how highly He regarded the baptizer.

Jesus' hearing about John's death wasn't just one of those, "Oh, that's too bad," moments. It's a good occasion for us to be reminded of how Jesus truly lived as the God-man He uniquely was. Even if by divine insight He knew this moment was coming, no doubt a wave of grief must have hit him, tearing at both His human compassion and divine heart.

The circumstances simply wouldn't allow Jesus to go and be present to grieve, as He would do later at the death of His friend Lazarus, with Lazarus' grieving sisters Mary and Martha. It was not the time or place for Jesus to perhaps get entangled with Herod and all that was involved in bringing about John's death. This same Herod would later play a small role in the fallacious trials of Jesus before He was crucified.

Some might also wonder why Jesus, who certainly had the power to raise the dead, didn't do for John what he was going to do for His friend Lazarus and others. Once again we're being drawn to the point John made when Jesus' ministry began to surpass his own. "He must increase, but I must decrease" (John 3:30). As unjust as John's death was, through faith we can see this was a part of God's sovereign plan to have Jesus' ministry be the one of greater import. All who study the Bible seriously gain the perspective that God's justice will, in due time, be served surely and exactly. The book of Revelation clearly depicts how those beheaded for Christ will be afforded special honor at God's throne in eternity. This will include those, like John, who were literally beheaded in their service to God, and generally to all who have suffered and died for the Lord and His kingdom.

So Jesus did what any of us would do if we knew we wanted and needed to grieve, but couldn't be there personally. He tried to get away, separated from the incredible demands His ministry was producing. Jesus and the disciples got away from the crowds, but only for a little while. I trust Jesus, somehow, somewhere, found some moments to experience and express, through thoughts or tears or both, His feeling of loss at the news of John's death. It's important to do so.

I know the story of a well-known gospel preacher whose wife died. He insisted there was to be no grieving of any kind. She had lived a wonderfully faithful life, and the preacher was adamant with family and friends there was to be only celebration—no tears or laments. And so it was. Then a week after his wife's funeral, the preacher experienced what might be called a nervous breakdown. Like this preacher and everyone else, even Jesus needed to grieve a significant loss.

I was good friends with all of my Bible professors at college. But with one, much older than the rest, I became particularly close. We continued to correspond after I had graduated and moved far away. He sent me one hand-written note that was particularly saturated with comments about God's grace, the predominant theme of his speaking and writing. Two weeks after I got the note, I learned that he had died of pneumonia. I was sorry to hear about his death, but I guess in the busyness of whatever I was doing at the moment, I somehow decided it wasn't important for me to grieve. A number of years passed, and I was studying and preaching out of Paul's second letter to Timothy, the one in which it's apparent Paul thinks his days will be few, and he's giving some very specific "final instructions" to the young preacher. With this on my mind, and I remember exactly where I was driving when this happened, I made the connection between Paul's letter to Timothy and the note I had received from brother K.C. Moser, one of my true heroes. I had to pull the car over and cry for a couple of minutes. I had finally gotten around to doing what I should have done years before—grieving for my friend. (By the way, that note is one of my most treasured possessions.) It's ironic that just two weeks after my moment of grieving for brother Moser, I got a call from my alma mater. They were informing me I had been selected to receive the annual award named in his honor. I was honored, humbled, and greatly relieved that I'd found the occasion and time to grieve for him, as I received that award.

At this point in the story, I wonder if you've developed the same admiration and even fondness for John, like so many Bible students have down through the centuries. Even though we see how he's greatly honored on the pages of Scripture, and we know we'll see him in Heaven, it's still okay if we feel a tinge of sadness as the reality of his unjust death sinks in.

We are told that after his death, some of John's disciples came and buried his body. I'm sure they grieved then and for a while. But interestingly, this one short verse about Jesus' trying to get away upon hearing of John's death is the Bible's only mention of any grieving on his behalf. Before the book concludes, I plan to come back with one more tribute and memorial to this man's life and death.

# 24

## THE AFTERMATH OF A GREAT LIFE

In this chapter we'll take brief looks at significant things said about John after his death. It's generally true that comments made about one after their passing sometimes have as much significance of things said by them or things said about them while they were still alive.

> *King Herod heard of it; for Jesus' name had become known. Some said, "John the baptizer has been raised from the dead; that is why these powers are at work in him." But others said, "It is Elijah." And others said, "It is a prophet, like one of the prophets of old." But when Herod heard of it he said, "John, whom I beheaded, has been raised." (Mark 6:14-16)*

This report on some believing the miracle-performing Jesus was actually John is reported twice in three of the gospel accounts. It's first given generally as the reasoning of people trying to somehow explain how Jesus was able to do what He was doing. Then in the second instance the same answer is offered by the disciples in direct response to a question from Jesus as to "Who do men say that I am?"

It's fascinating how the people of that region and Herod himself should so readily concoct a hypothesis attributing Jesus' powers to a supposed resurrection of John from the dead. The Jewish people were divided religiously on the matter of whether or not there would be some kind of general resurrection of the dead at the end of time. More likely these thoughts came from some underlying beliefs and practices in that culture that were akin to what we'd today call the occult. This may have been particularly true for Herod. It's like the seemingly endless fascination ours and many other cultures have with the stories of vampires. In those stories often one or more characters have assumed some post-death existence wherein they live on, often with some degree of supernatural powers.

I'm struck with how adamant Herod is in stating his belief (as erroneous as it was) about who Jesus was. We saw Herod before, conflicted and sorrowful at the baptizer's death. Now notice him confidently saying, "It's John, whom I beheaded." People who have no real moral compass often change their tune from the sniveling creatures they actually were in some instance, if they think it's to their advantage, to taking the credit for some action, albeit noble or dastardly.

> *You sent to John as he bore witness to the truth. Not that the testimony which I receive is from man; but I say this that you may be saved. He was a burning and shining lamp, and you were willing to rejoice for a while in his light. But the testimony which I have is greater than that of John; for the works which the Father has granted me to accomplish, these very works which I am doing, bear me witness that the Father has sent me. (John 5:33-36)*

Before we conclude our study, we'll see Jesus several times citing something about John to make a point in His teaching. Here he appeals to the people who put their trust in John as a source of truth. This in no way diminishes anything about John, but in fact enhances our understanding and appreciation of him as the "forerunner" of the Christ. The listeners to both of these preachers were stunned at the truthfulness and authoritativeness of their messages, as compared to the traditions and teachings of men they had been hearing from their scribes and teachers of the Law. Jesus is saying, in effect, you believed John; I have even a greater witness to the truthfulness of what I am saying, the Father Himself.

If some parts of either John's or Jesus' messages had been identified as false (really false, not just accusations of falsehood by those who themselves were distorting the truth), then the ministries of both would have collapsed. All of us who preach the Word should be most concerned about one crucial thing, more than our speaking ability, or personal charisma, or even our grammar and syntax. Is what we are preaching the truth?

> **He went away again across the Jordan to the place where John at first baptized, and there he remained. And many came to him; and they said, "John did no sign, but everything that John said about this man was true." And many believed in him there. (John 10:40-42)**

Just as we see Jesus at times appealing to the truthfulness of John's testimony about Himself, here we see the people themselves coming to the same conclusion. It is not hard to infer from this statement that the people were realizing that while John wasn't a miracle worker as was Jesus, the things John had said about Jesus were nonetheless true. Now Jesus, another speaker of truth, has all of these signs, wonders and miracles to even give more testimony (verification) to the truthfulness and power of the message.

It's noteworthy that John, who had been full of the Spirit from when he was in his mother's womb, never performed any miracles. Yet even without the miracles, his message had rung true in the hearts of multitudes. The power of John's words was great. The power of Jesus' words and His working of signs (miracles) was even greater!

# 25

## SIMILARITIES TO JESUS

> *Now when Jesus came into the district of Caesarea Philippi, he asked his disciples, "Who do men say that the Son of man is?" And they said, "Some say John the Baptist, others say Elijah, and others Jeremiah or one of the prophets." (Matt. 16:13-14)*

This is the introduction to the well-known story where Jesus polls His disciples for what people are generally thinking about Him, and then turns the same question directly to those disciples. This is where Peter makes his famous confession of Christ, followed by a glowing commendation to Peter personally and a promise to all the apostles. The passage continues with Jesus predicting his suffering, death, and resurrection in or around Jerusalem. Then an equally non-glowing statement by Peter prompts a stinging rebuke by Jesus, and there are some classic teachings by Jesus about the essence of what it means to be a disciple of His.

Since we've already noticed some people, including Herod himself who had played a key role in John's death, attributing Jesus' miracle-working abilities to Him being John raised from the dead, we're not surprised to see this same report being given as a part of the disciples' answer to this question.

If we're going to fully appreciate John, a key part of that would have to be noticing his similarities to the person of Jesus, who by John's several declarations is one whose preeminence is absolute.

Let's start to consider the confusion regarding these two by the simple fact that obviously those in the land had nothing equivalent to things we have in our "communication age." Knowledge of anything was gained by first-hand observation, or more likely by word-of-mouth. So without newspapers, photography, television, telephones, cell phones and the Internet, there could neither be direct tracking of where these two preachers were all the time, nor any side-by-side comparisons as we commonly see today. Additionally, solely depending on word-of-mouth commonly lent itself to a "rumor mill" that usually ended up confusing or even wildly distorting the facts of anything.

Here are some other fairly common ways in which John and Jesus could have been confused:

- They were about the same age.
- Being related to each other, they could have looked very much alike.
- By John's wilderness lifestyle and Jesus' being a carpenter, both had a rugged, outdoorsman kind of appearance.
- They both seemed to have a rather natural charisma that attracted people.
- The subject of "repentance" was very much a part of the preaching of both of them.
- People being baptized was readily associated with each of their ministries.
- Both were not reluctant to be bold and "tell it like it is" in reference to sin or hypocrisy.
- Some who had been disciples of John had now become disciples of Jesus.

The confusion of Jesus being John (by now that would have to be a resurrected John) is nothing but flattering to Jesus, as was His being identified with great Old Testament characters Elijah, Jeremiah, or one of the prophets.

Likewise, it is flattering to Jesus that the disciples' answer of what people were saying (really what they were thinking) didn't include some scoundrels, hypocrites, or even of the self-acclaimed "messiahs" that seemed ever-present during this time-frame.

From this point it probably didn't take long for most to figure out that John was dead and that Jesus was carrying on an even greater ministry in His own right.

But for our purposes in this book, trying to understand more about John, it is likewise flattering to be associated, if even at first in confusion, with the Christ. As we've seen, the work of John was a true precursor to the work of Jesus. Even though eventually the knowledge of Christ would greatly surpass any about John, we can appreciate how their lives and ministries were and always will be inseparably linked.

# 26

## JESUS ON JOHN

We shall look briefly at three statements made by Jesus about John, with some time having passed since John's death. Although not yet a part of the lore of other prominent and faithful Old Testament figures, Jesus' natural references to John as He taught tell us both of Jesus' great respect for John in the work of God on earth, and give a preview of John's place in the Scriptures when they would be completed.

> *And as they were coming down the mountain, Jesus commanded them, "Tell no one the vision, until the Son of man is raised from the dead." And the disciples asked him, "Then why do the scribes say that first Elijah must come?" He replied, "Elijah does come, and he is to restore all things; but I tell you that Elijah has already come, and they did not know him, but did to him whatever they pleased. So also the Son of man will suffer at their hands." Then the disciples understood that he was speaking to them of John the Baptist. (Matt. 17:9-13)*

Peter, James, and John had just witnessed the absolutely unique transfiguration of Christ. Nothing like it had or will ever happen again on this earth! Among the several miracles occurring within that spectacular event was the appearance of Moses and Elijah with Jesus, thus representing the Law, the Prophets and now, as so deemed by the very voice of God, Jesus, the One who was to be most honored.

In the course of their descent, the apostles asked Jesus something any typically trained Jewish man would have asked. They asked about the coming of Elijah in reference to the timing of the Messiah (or Christ). We've already considered the prophecies related to this coming of Elijah, and how John had fulfilled them exactly. But here's this additional affirming by Jesus that indeed Elijah has come, representatively, was not totally believed, and suffered as all other prophets seemed doomed to do. With some time to have considered Jesus' earlier statements tying Elijah with John, these sometimes slow to grasp disciples seem to rather easily realize Jesus was speaking to them about John. It's just one more time we see Jesus giving honor and commendation to John.

> *"Truly, I say to you, the tax collectors and the harlots go into the kingdom of God before you. For John came to you in the way of righteousness, and you did not believe him, but the tax collectors and the harlots believed him; and even when you saw it, you did not afterward repent and believe it." (Matt. 21:31-32)*

This passage occurs within the greater context of Jesus' parable of the two sons. When asked by their father to work for him on a certain day, the first son had said, "I will not," but later changed his mind and worked. The second son had said, "I will," but didn't do it. Jesus' point is how some you'd expect to be doing the will of God somehow don't, while those you might least expect are the ones who end up pleasing God. He makes use of two groups of people upon which the average Jewish listener would look with disdain—the tax collectors (Jews who had sold out and were working for the despised Roman occupiers), and the harlots (then and now considered a most unholy profession).

But in the midst of this teaching, Jesus just happens to mention John, specifically as one who "came in the way of righteousness." The Jews who couldn't bring themselves to accept Jesus as the Messiah, in spite of the fact that no one wanted to dispute the righteousness of John, also hadn't accepted and obeyed John. But in spite of the seemingly undisputed righteousness of John, it was these despised tax collectors and harlots who heard John and believed him.

The unspoken irony in this illustration by Jesus is that like the forerunner John, Jesus and His message had also been accepted by those considered "sinners" by the self-righteous. This, in fact, was one of their chief complaints against Jesus, how He consorted with these undesirables. Woven throughout the gospels is the theme that those who would assume they are unquestionably shoe-ins to be a part of the kingdom are shocked to learn they aren't, while many who would have been deemed as having no chance will be let in.

Jesus' commendation of John as one who came in righteousness is indeed noteworthy. But there's an even more subtle truth in this and related accounts for those who will think beyond the obvious. The preaching of first John and then Jesus would have been considered by many to be too harsh, or perhaps too plainspoken about certain sins. Some then and now would think they should have perhaps toned down their rhetoric, being careful not to say anything that would offend. Neither toned it down, and guess who flocked to them anyway? Those considered beyond the reach of God because of their sinfulness. John and Jesus were quite similar in more ways than we've realized.

> **And as he was walking in the temple, the chief priests and the scribes and the elders came to him, and they said to him, "By what authority are you doing these things, or who gave you this authority to do them?" Jesus said to them, "I will ask you a question; answer me,**

*and I will tell you by what authority I do these things. Was the baptism of John from heaven or from men? Answer me." And they argued with one another, "If we say, 'From Heaven,' he will say, "Why then did you not believe him? But shall we say, 'From men'?" – they were afraid of the people, for all held that John was a real prophet. So they answered Jesus, "We do not know." And Jesus said to them, "Neither will I tell you by what authority I do these things." (Mark 11:27-33)*

This passage's primary purpose is to show Jesus' superiority of logic and skill over what turned out to be these hapless and fearful questioners. But tucked within the encounter, we see Jesus once again using John as a known and respected figure. For them, regrettably, those challenging Jesus were more fearful of what the people around them might think, and not caring so much for what was right before the Lord.

# 27

## CHRIST SUPERSEDING

By the time we get to the book of Acts, since there's been some time between John's death and the end of Jesus' earthly ministry, we might assume we'd hear little of John, except maybe an occasional reminder of the value of his life and service to God.

In light of the fact that John himself had made it clear of the greater and longer lasting effects of Jesus' ministry as compared to his own, we might trust all of his disciples had gotten the message, and appropriately shifted their allegiance to Christ. With that change to following Jesus would have been an acceptance and teaching of Christ's doctrines on all matters, including baptism. But while that may have been the case there in Palestine (Judea, Samaria, and Galilee), we will notice that in more far-flung places, the practice of John's baptism lived on.

Bible students should learn to recognize the sometimes subtle but significant changes that occur when an activity by God, or a covenant, or a "law" has been fulfilled or surpassed by whatever God wants to happen next. As a Christian I can look at and appreciate all of the different arrangements, covenants, or laws under which God's people were to follow Him. Scripture makes it clear that the basic nature of God doesn't change. But that doesn't mean that I am obligated to keep any of those former laws, since I am now under the "New Covenant" and the law of Christ. Christians are now a part of God's family by their "new birth," and not just by birth into a particular nation.

Things that have remained constant with these changes are God's sovereignty and concern for His people, and the necessity of faith by those trying to follow Him. What doesn't always remain the same is how people are to respond to Him in obedience to Him, how they are to worship, and to some extent how they may live their daily lives.

Shortly after the passion (suffering) of Christ, His resurrection, His appearances to the apostles and others, and His ascension to Heaven, the next major change for God-followers came with the establishment of the church (see Acts 2). This happened on the Jewish feast day, the Day of Pentecost, which occurred fifty days after Jesus had been raised from the dead. Jesus had promised to build His church (Matt. 16:18), and that construction continues to this day. Newly baptized believers were "added" to the church by the Lord on that first day (Acts 2:41, 47). Every time since, when someone believes and obeys the gospel, they likewise are added to His church. In 1 Peter 2:4-10 the apostle describes this in another way. As people come to Jesus, the "living stone," they also, like "living stones" are being built into a worshiping and serving "priesthood," which now encompasses all Christians. Paul conveys the same imagery as he talks about Christ as the "chief cornerstone," and how the church rises to become a (spiritual, not physical) temple in the Lord (see Eph. 2:19-22).

Inherent in the preaching and teaching that was to occur in this new church age was the principle of people being baptized "in Jesus' name." We first see that in Jesus' giving what we now call "the great commission" (Matt. 28:19-20). He taught that His disciples were to make other disciples, and a part of that included them being baptized in the name of the Father, the Son, and the Holy Spirit. Peter reiterated in his sermon on the Day of Pentecost that every one of those who had heard the message of Christ and had been cut (or pricked) to the heart should repent and be baptized "in the name of Jesus Christ" (Acts 2:38).

Seeing this does raise a subtle but important difference in the baptism that was to be administered and received in the church age, as compared to the baptisms that had occurred before, i.e. the baptism administered by John, and then later by Jesus' disciples during His ministry. This also usually raises the question as to whether or not those baptized in those previous baptisms now needed to be re-baptized in this new baptism into Christ (see Rom. 6:3 and Gal. 3:27 for references to "baptized into Christ").

[NOTE: For simplicity's sake from this point forward I will distinguish being baptized in Jesus' name as "Christian baptism," in contrast to "John's baptism."]

I say "new baptism" because while there are similarities, there are also some significant differences. Although the texts don't always specifically include the words "believe" or "faith," it's very clear that it was acceptance and trust in the messages they were hearing that prompted people to repent and be baptized. The principle of repentance is clearly seen in both John's and Christian baptism. The accounts of those being baptized with John's baptism and for Christian baptism are "for the forgiveness of sins" (see Mark 1:4 and Acts 2:38).

While John frequently spoke of the one coming after him, for whom he was the forerunner, we never see that any of his baptizing was "in Jesus' name." If you are familiar with the early part of Acts, you'll remember there are frequent references to what is being done "in Jesus' name." At any time in history, but especially there in the first century, certain names carried or represented authority (or, power). Remember also that we have several places where we're instructed to pray "in Jesus' name." Paul told the Colossians that whatever they did, in word or deed, to do it all in the name of the Lord Jesus (see Col. 3:17).

Paul tells us in Ephesians 1:3 that all spiritual blessings are "in

Christ." Christian baptism is to be in the name of Christ, and we are baptized into Christ. John's baptism afforded its recipients certain spiritual blessings, but not all as does Christian baptism. Two very important ones that come readily to mind are "the gift of the Holy Spirit" (Acts 2:38) and being added to the church (Acts. 2:41, 47).

So the very practical question that arises when we consider all of this, and surely more expediently needed to be answered in the early church is, "Did those who received John's baptism now also need to receive Christian baptism? Yes, in the former they had also received "remission of sins," but there are any number of blessings they would have missed had they received only the former.

# 28

## KNEW ONLY JOHN'S BAPTISM

> *Now a Jew named Apollos, a native of Alexandria, came to Ephesus. He was an eloquent man, well versed in the scriptures. He had been instructed in the way of the Lord; and being fervent in spirit, he spoke and taught accurately the things concerning Jesus, though he knew only the baptism of John. He began to speak boldly in the synagogue; but when Priscilla and Aquila heard him, they took him and expounded to him the way of God more accurately. (Acts 18:24-26)*

We wish we knew the story of how Apollos got to where he was in his faith when this section begins. He is a Jew with a Greek name from Alexandria. In other words he's quite cosmopolitan. Where and how he had become a Christ-follower is not revealed. He had a résumé most preachers would envy. (Many congregations today in need of a preacher are drooling for a guy like this.) Just consider his attributes:

- He was eloquent (in other words, he could "wow" them as a speaker).
- He was well educated, especially in the Scriptures.

- He spoke with passion and boldness.
- He spoke the truth about Jesus.

(Oh, there's that one little thing, but nobody's perfect, right?)

The one thing Luke records for us that was amiss in this powerful speaker "is he knew only the baptism of John." That seems almost unimaginable at this point, so removed from John by time and miles. As has already been said, many today would fully accept this type of speaker without qualms, reasoning like so many do today about spiritual matters, "Four out of five ain't bad!" This would be especially the case in regards to a matter such as baptism, since so many divergent views exist about everything from mode to purpose to prerequisites for its administration.

But it wasn't something to be ignored by listeners Aquila and Priscilla. They were the evangelistically-minded couple that had teamed with Paul briefly as a tent-maker, but more importantly they became a part of the network of young evangelists and other dedicated workers Paul was using to spread the gospel throughout that part of the world.

The fact that this couple noticed and were concerned about the deficiency in Apollos' teaching is, in my consideration, surpassed by how they chose to address the situation. Some would have let what should have been taught be compromised. Others might have addressed Apollos harshly, perhaps even on the spot, and the results might not have been as good. As it was they invited him to their home and we see that classic phrase of how they "expounded to him the way of God more accurately." That's another of those Bible stories where we wish we had more detail. I choose to think they must have been both gentle and effective with Apollos, as he becomes a solid part of the Lord's work from that point on.

Remember that the point of concern is what some would consider a subtle difference about baptism. This takes on even more importance when we consider that Paul, in his well-known seven "ones" of unity, one of those is "one baptism" (see Eph. 4:5). Sadly, in today's badly divided Christendom, there's anything but a consensus about what this "one baptism" is. While that study is not the purpose of this book, let's take note to understand the Biblical accuracy of what we teach and share with others in a loving way is very important.

> *While Apollos was at Corinth, Paul passed through the upper country and came to Ephesus. There he found some disciples. And he said to them, "Did you receive the Holy Spirit when you believed?" And they said, "No, we have never even heard that there is a Holy Spirit." And he said, "Into what then were you baptized?" They said, "Into John's baptism." And Paul said, "John baptized with the baptism of repentance, telling the people to believe in the one who was to come after him, that is, Jesus." On hearing this, they were baptized in the name of the Lord Jesus. And when Paul had laid his hands upon them, the Holy Spirit came on them; and they spoke with tongues and prophesied. There were about twelve of them in all. (Acts 19:1-7)*

We have another example of those still limited by their only knowing of John's baptism. Apollos remained at Corinth, and Paul traveled to Ephesus. There he found these twelve people. Let's try to understand the story in its own right, but also of how it might affect some with whom we would interact today.

First it mentions they were "disciples." We could wrangle all day about whether or not this meant they were disciples of John. Their lack of knowledge about the Holy Spirit would make it unlikely they were Jews, for while the Spirit is not mentioned as much in the Old Testament, it can be clearly seen in key places of the Old Testament. It's possible they could have learned about Jesus, and were in the very earliest stages of being "made disciples" by someone. But if that's the case, one wonders way they knew nothing of being baptized in Jesus' name, but only knew of the baptism of John. All we can deduct is what they believed at that time, but they were taught about both Christian baptism and the Holy Spirit by Paul.

What happens in short order, first, they were baptized in Jesus' name. Then, as what had been happening in the early church, Paul, as an apostle, laid his hands on them. They received, as can be seen in other places and some of the letters, this apostolic laying on of hands, which prompted two areas of miraculous giftedness through the Holy Spirit. First they were able to speak in "tongues" (another language which they had never learned). Then they "prophesied," which can mean anything from just preaching or teaching with special help from the Spirit to actually foretelling of coming events through the Spirit's assistance.

These two stories should either teach or remind all of us something of great importance. When encountering some who had partial knowledge of Christian baptism, those first century Christians were not hesitant at all to try to correct the misunderstanding and show them, among other things, which baptism they were to receive. This is a constant challenge when we today come upon people who love the Lord, but were taught either a man-made doctrine about baptism. As has been previously stated, this should be done "with great patience and careful instruction." Conducting such studies with those untaught should never be dictated by human traditions or merely opinions, but on the truth found in the Scriptures.

Thus ends our study of John and how he lived a life of devotion, courage, and nonconformity. Jesus is still our ultimate example, but we should also learn and be motivated by others in the Scripture who faithfully served the Lord. I pray you have not only come to know or increase your knowledge of John the Baptist, but perhaps also see him in a more personalized way.

Don't forget to read the epilogue which follows. It is my attempt to honor John in a special way.

# EPILOGUE

EXPLANATORY NOTE: John's death is recorded in Scripture without a lot of explanation or fanfare. Later Jesus said some very commending things about John and his ministry. I have written a dramatization, based on my understanding of key Scriptures, of things he experienced and the kinds of things I hope we all will experience as we leave this life. I realize there are many interpretations of what happens to a soul after death, and also related "end times" matters. For now let's just rejoice, trusting God will do exactly the right things to receive and reward His faithful ones.

Before us we see the gruesome scene of John's beheading. But immediately after his death John was escorted by angels to Paradise. Those same angels had been invisibly surrounding him and his work throughout his life, but he was now seeing them for the first time. He instantly felt totally at peace as he was carried away from that horrific situation by these warm and comforting heavenly creatures.

Paradise, as the name implies, is the wonderful place for those happily awaiting the judgment. Paradise is where Jesus had promised a thief he'd be later that day, as they were both being crucified. It's also where the beggar Lazarus was taken.

Upon his arrival John, like all those who are "asleep in the Lord," was already seeing and experiencing things beyond what any mortal on earth can imagine. If there had been any misconception about somehow bypassing the judgment and going directly to Heaven, it was more than displaced by the incredible beauty and comfort of this place. John, like so many before him and myriads after, had been wondrously transferred from his earthly travail to an incredible spiritual place.

Everyone in Paradise, including John, was now fully cognizant they would someday go to Heaven. John and all the others there in Paradise gladly accepted that in the light of eternity, the wait would not be long. We're not sure if John and the others were or weren't aware of another place—Hades—where others now passed from life on earth were waiting for judgment. These are those who are not in the Lord. Their fate would be the total opposite of Heaven. It would be in the place called Hell, and hellish it would be in every way. If those in Paradise knew about Hades, it didn't in the least take away from their great pleasure.

John was welcomed by all the godly men and women of all time. It was like the grandest and sweetest homecoming ever, only to be surpassed when all of these would someday go into Heaven. While no one in Paradise really outranked anyone else, John somehow instantly recognized all of his heroes from Scripture. Delightfully he felt as if he was in the very bosom of Abraham. He and Elijah in particular had a lot to talk about! That's what seemed to go on endlessly: meeting, greeting, embracing, exchanging holy kisses, and discussing with joy and celebration all the things that had gone on before.

Some had anticipated John's arrival for a long time. Others seemed somehow to be internally informed of who he was, and what his role had been in God's plan on earth. All seemed satisfied. All seemed to rejoice in each other's presence, whether their life and faith story from earth had been recorded in Scripture or not.

It wasn't just those who had gone before that John got to meet.

Almost every moment brought more arrivals. The incomparable joy of John's reception was repeated with each new arrival. Everyone seemed eager to meet and greet everyone else, but no one felt like they had to be in a hurry to do so.

After a little while, more of the new arrivals seemed to already know about John. Many told him how much knowing his story had affected their own faith walk. John seemed equally eager to hear about how they had come to be God's child and had lived for Him during their sojourn on earth.

Sweet beyond comprehension was the joy everyone manifested not only towards those who had lived faithfully for the Lord while on earth, but for those who had never been given that chance. These included the ones the Father had mercifully taken from their mother's wombs before they were born, or early in their lives. Then there were also the myriads whose lives had been wantonly ended by human choice. They were referred to as "the innocents." There they were, not as infants or children but as full-grown adults, beaming and beautiful, enjoying their rightful place in Paradise. (As I write this I think of my own grandchild who none of us ever got to meet, but will get to talk with someday. Maybe you're thinking of someone like that, or just some of those who never really had a loving parent or grandparent. Won't it be grand!)

Then at some point the scene shifts to a glorious day, the "Day of the Lord" that everyone seemed to know was coming. In what seemed no longer than a twinkle of the eye, everyone in Paradise was immediately surrounding Jesus. He had come from Heaven and was in the sky above earth with a host of His mighty angels. What happened next occurred so quickly that John and the others could hardly grasp it all as it unfolded! The spirits that had come from Paradise were being miraculously reunited with their bodies from earth. Yes, out of graves and the sea and everywhere else—though many had been dead for thousands of years, their bodies were being remade and raised to this happy throng in the air, with Jesus at the very center of it. John's old body was being made into a new eternal body, with his head intact!

The spectacle which followed was almost inconceivable. Suddenly all the faithful then living on earth were rising from whatever they were doing to join the Lord, the angels, and those who had been asleep in Jesus. Everyone seemed to exult in the knowledge that this being with the Lord was going to last forever!

From there the whole company was transported to a great scene, complete with a great white throne, just outside the gates of Heaven. There were two groups of people gathered in front of that throne. It was like a great separation of the sheep and the goats. A smaller group was constituted of those who had, sometimes without realizing all of its import, served the Lord faithfully while on earth. But opposite the flock of the faithful was another larger group—those who had chosen not to serve the Lord at all, or in the way He had prescribed. Even though the judgment and pronouncements had not yet been made, those people seemed to sense which side of the equation they were on. While John and his peers were experiencing great joy, for the others there was only incomparable heartache.

At that great judgment scene some from "the goats" protested their placement. Others didn't seem to understand why they were where they were, either for the better or for the worst eventual placement. King Jesus listened and ruled. Finally many were told to "depart," while some were told to "enter in." What happened next was a glorious entry into Heaven by the faithful—the ultimate and final homecoming. A thought in seeing this was how it made the entry of the Olympians at their opening ceremony, which had to be one of earth's more glorious moments, pale in comparison to the ovation of the angels!

Finally, all are at God's throne, the center point of Heaven. There was the Father, Jesus the Lamb, the seven-fold Spirit of God, the angels and heavenly creatures, and the twenty-four elders casting down their golden crowns. All of God's redeemed from all time were there around the throne, rejoicing and praising their God, His Son, and the Spirit. There also, in a special place of recognition and honor, were the souls of those who had been beheaded for the testimony to Jesus and for the word of God. Of course, there was John among them. Everyone who saw this special honor was pleased. There wasn't a hint of jealousy for those in that special place; everyone understood. After all, each soul present, though perhaps not actually beheaded for Christ, had in their own way suffered for Him—it was just a part of their journey.

# ACKNOWLEDGMENTS

I have been greatly blessed to have some friends who have served as "pre-readers" for this book. I asked each of them to do this because of their love of the Lord and His Word. Their hours of pouring over this material, in its various stages, and their invaluable suggestions, are so deeply appreciated.

Janice Casey - Texas
Leigh Anne Delk – Texas
Dixie Hawkey – South Dakota
Chip Hartzell – North Carolina
Weldon McKinney – Texas
Joyce Webb – Virginia
Lawanna Woods - Texas

Made in the USA
Middletown, DE
31 March 2021